I0072821

Your Next Inspiration

IDEAS FOR FUNDRAISING AND GRANTMAKING

JOHN ROBINSON

CFPC PRESS, LLC

TABLE *of* CONTENTS

PART TWO: GRANTMAKING IDEAS

INTRODUCTION

SINCE JULY 27, 1980, I have had the privilege of working for and representing the Amon G. Carter Foundation in Fort Worth. I have been asked numerous times how I got what seems to be one of the greatest jobs in the world—giving away money. Well, the summer before my senior year in high school, Texas Christian University recruited me to be an accounting major with the pitch, "Whatever you do in life, accounting will be part of it." They went on to say, come to TCU, major in accounting, make good grades, and "We *guarantee* you will be offered a job by a public accounting firm. Public accounting will provide one career path, but what will probably happen is you will meet a client in a business you have never heard of. You will like them, they will like you, and that is where you will go." Which is exactly what happened to me.

The Carter Foundation hired me on the accounting/investment side with no promise of my ever doing anything else. Looking back, several amazing things fell into place that helped prepare me for the transition to responsibility for grantmaking.

The Foundation had seven employees when I started, so job descriptions were pretty vague. I was responsible for the monthly accounting reports and preparing the year-end Form 990-PF tax return. The Carter family also operated a smaller foundation, the Amon G. Carter Star-Telegram Employees Fund, which I was asked to help administer. It wasn't too long before I was invited to be on a new United Way "venture grants" committee, which was my first exposure to creative grantmaking. I ended up doing more extensive volunteer work for United Way, including chairing the Allocations Committee, where I was introduced to social service programming and budgeting and got to meet the leaders of these critical organizations.

Since 1997, the Carter Foundation directors have allowed me to represent the Foundation and meet with all of the organizations seeking grant support. During this time our annual grant budget has grown from $15 million to nearly $40 million. Even with this significant increase it has remained our approach to meet with all organizations we consider funding.

I am amused that most calls for appointments are requests for "advice" rather than funding. I realize the logic is surely a foundation officer is more likely to fund their own advice to help it be successful. My preference is to first learn about an organization's plans, ask questions, and share what others have done in hope of introducing new ideas. My objective is not for them to duplicate someone else's strategy but rather modify it to fit their situation.

As an example, back in the early 2000s I was president of the Conference of Southwest Foundations (now Philanthropy Southwest). During one annual meeting we had a session titled Thirty Ideas in Sixty Minutes that let member foundations share unique funding experiences. A Phoenix funder presented that each year they assisted a local food bank. He went on to say his foundation realized families who did not have enough money to feed themselves certainly did not have the resources to feed their pets. So, they designated some of their grant money to go toward the purchase of pet food to include with the people food delivery.

That was a good idea! The thought that immediately occurred to me was if food pantries know the size of the families and possibly the ages of their children, why not include books along with the food distribution. The Phoenix funder never mentioned literacy but that idea stimulated a new avenue of thinking for me.

After 25-plus years and making more than 5,000 grants, I have shared ideas with a number of people and many have encouraged me to "write a book." Since one of my core desires is to help others help themselves, this book is my effort to share ideas and examples and motivate a broader fundraising and grantmaking audience.

Even the format of this book is an example of how concepts develop. My vision of sharing ideas did not lend itself to traditional chapters but the layout inspiration came from a how-to masterpiece—Harvey Penick's *Little Red Book*—a compilation from years of teaching others how to play golf. Similarly, I want to share examples of creative grantmaking and fundraising (although not all will apply in every situation). These brief ideas hopefully will ignite fundraising and grantmaking ideas, and encourage individuals wishing to have a greater impact.

In his will Amon G. Carter said, "I have come to realize that they who acquire wealth are more or less stewards in the application of that wealth to others of the human family who are less fortunate than themselves. The hand that in life grips with a miser's clutch and the ear that refuses to heed the pleading voice of humanity forfeits the most precious of all gifts of earth and heaven—the happiness within the heart that comes from doing good to others."

My career is a testament that there is no greater joy than helping people. May this book inspire you to do the same.

Part One

Fundraising Ideas

LOOKING FOR AND FINDING INSPIRATION

IF YOU WERE to ask someone, "How many red cars did you see while driving around today?" the response likely would be, "I have no idea, I wasn't looking for red cars." But follow up with, "How about I pay you for every red car you see tomorrow," and that person will absolutely be looking for red cars! Opportunities and inspirations are something you should always watch for even if you're not being paid to do so.

An entrepreneurial friend, Elliot Goldman, received a Heifer International catalog in the mail. Heifer International is a global nonprofit working to eradicate poverty and hunger through sustainable, values-based holistic community development. Contributions purchase animals, provide agricultural education and value-based training, and help families in need around the world move toward self-sufficiency.

After looking through the mailing, Elliot was inspired to take the Heifer model and create *The Greatest Gift Catalog Ever*. This publication highlighted local nonprofits and their programs along with examples of what a contribution of $25, $50, $100 or more could provide the organization. Seventeen years later, *The Greatest Gift Catalog Ever* generates more than $1 million in annual contributions to its highlighted charities. Nonprofits compete to be included in the annual publication. Even more impressive, the model has been replicated in other cities.

Everyone should always be alert to ideas that can be modified to fit their situation. The following pages will help get you started finding your next inspiration. Think of it as a metaphorical parking lot of red cars! ♀

REACHING NEW AUDIENCES

The Taste Project

JEFF AND JULIE WILLIAMS have a heart for addressing food insecurity. Instead of the traditional food pantry/soup kitchen, they opened The Taste Project restaurant using an unconventional business model—offer a seasonal menu of locally sourced food more likely found in an upscale bistro. But with a twist: The menu didn't show any prices; diners were encouraged to pay only what they could, or pay what they would for a similar meal in a comparable restaurant, or even pay something extra to help offset the uncovered expenses inherent in this approach.

Nowhere in the restaurant or on the "bill" (which only listed what was ordered) were there any payment guidelines or suggested amounts. The wait staff were volunteers, so tipping was not a factor, and all receipts went toward the cause. The Taste Project had been open just a few months when Jeff and Julie came to see me. After discussing their start-up experience and learning more about how things worked, I told them our Foundation was not a good candidate for operating support. They said they understood but had heard that in addition to funding we often (sometimes) had good ideas.

My immediate thought was Celebrity Waiters. Up until then, all advertising had been social media and word of mouth. I suggested they ask high-profile people they knew to invite others in their sphere of influence to come have a meal at the restaurant and be waited on by them. I thought they might try this once as a pilot effort to gauge logistics and the need for reservations, parking, etc. Instead, Jeff and Julie lined up an array of prominent people for every Thursday in September from various backgrounds, including their City Council representative, the Fort Worth Symphony conductor, a TV personality, the area's promotion and development arm, and the TCU women's basketball team. Some pilot!

When Jeff and Julie reported their plans back to me they also said they "might" have mentioned (since it was my idea) that the Foundation would match whatever was raised on celebrity days. We did put some parameters that limited the match to $1,000 per person in case some highly competitive type got a bank trust department to make a big gift. As for results, up until then, typical days generated $900–$1,100 in revenue. On celebrity days, receipts jumped to between $6,000 and $7,000 and our match generated another $25,000 for the month. I told them that was a fantastic response, but the true measure of success would be if these diners continued to return. I am happy to report their approach has worked and a second location has recently opened.

Celebrity Waiters continues to be a successful strategy for The Taste Project with different groups of high-profile individuals volunteering, including some repeaters. Another unanticipated result was the CEO of a local hospital started bringing administrative groups to volunteer as a team building exercise. Jeff and Julie Williams have made presentations around the country to similar groups that have been inspired to adopt the Celebrity Waiter approach. ♀

REACHING NEW AUDIENCES

Carter BloodCare

IT'S FASCINATING TO see how ideas can spur creativity. I was sharing The Taste Project Celebrity Waiter story with the Carter BloodCare leadership team. The Carter name is not coincidental, since the Foundation helped start the Carter Blood Center in the 1950s. Through strategic mergers Carter BloodCare has grown to provide blood service for over 150 hospitals and medical facilities in a region that spans 50 Texas counties.

As soon as their CEO heard the example, he said, "We can do that! We will recruit celebrity blood donors throughout the communities we serve to reach out and promote the need to donate blood." Mayors, sheriffs, chiefs of police and CEOs in communities throughout the service region promote blood donations using their celebrity. I never would have thought a Celebrity Waiter story would translate to healthcare, but that is the power of ideas and how they can be adapted to multiple situations. ♀

STEPS TO INCREASED GIVING

United Way of Tarrant County

UNITED WAY HAS a long history of being a critical funder in most communities. In Fort Worth/Tarrant County a strong push emerged to grow the Alexis de Tocqueville Society, which recognized individuals who contribute at least $10,000 per year to its Annual Campaign.

To help execute a strategy that would expand this group of donors, United Way identified individuals with the capacity to give at this level and proposed an offer to the Foundation: If a donor would commit to contributing $5,000 in year one, $7,500 in year two and $10,000 in year three, would the Carter Foundation match the first-year $5,000 payment and then fund $2,500 upon receipt of the pledge payment in year two? This would bring each year's annual contribution to $10,000. Donors agreeing to the three-year commitment would be recognized as de Tocqueville members the first year with no asterisk indicating how the giving tier was achieved. The program worked very well!

Long term, it would be United Way's job to keep these generous givers engaged with a deeper understanding of the impact they were making. Obviously, they were recognized in all reports as members of the prestigious Alexis de Tocqueville Society. In my experience donors who become engaged over a multi-year (3+) period are much easier to retain than those who respond to just a one-time incentive. ♀

STEPS TO INCREASED GIVING

Big Brothers Big Sisters Lone Star

DURING A FUNDRAISING discussion with Big Brothers Big Sisters Lone Star, I shared the success United Way had with its multi-year stair step matching appeal. It wasn't long before Big Brothers Big Sisters came back with their version for a similar challenge. Their proposal was to identify new donors willing to commit $10,000 over three years—$2,000, then $3,000, then $5,000—hoping we would match $3,000 in year one and $2,000 in year two. Big Brothers Big Sisters put a further requirement on themselves that they would not earn the match unless they added 100 new donors.

One feature of the plan I particularly liked was Big Brothers Big Sisters tailored the strategy to meet their situation, board and staff capability, and self-imposed a high threshold to earn the grant. They actually exceeded the goal with commitments from 120 new donors, that generated $600,000 in new donations for each of the three years, which meant I had to go back to the Carter Board to get approval for an even larger match.

Another aspect of this grant that makes it one of my favorites is Big Brothers took the results of this model to several smaller communities around Texas. Building on their success with our grant, they secured local funders to match similar multi-year appeals that were scaled to community capability such as finding individuals willing to commit $1,000 the first year, $2,000 the second year and $3,000 in the third. Developing a base level of reliable support for future years was extremely beneficial in helping plan their program delivery. ♀

STEPS TO INCREASED GIVING

Fort Worth Symphony Orchestra

ONE FINAL EXAMPLE of multi-year support involves the Fort Worth Symphony Orchestra. The Symphony suffered through an acrimonious strike, and many of the musicians had friends sign petitions in support of their demands for higher pay and benefits. Once the strike was settled, I approached Symphony leadership with a proposal that the musicians should go back to all of these petition-signing individuals and solicit their support.

The Foundation offered to provide up to $500,000 as a match for all new or increased gifts up to $10,000 per year, providing the donor would commit to a three-year pledge. The only restriction was anyone already contributing more than $10,000 was not eligible for the match.

My thinking was, long term, the Symphony would be healthier with a broader base of supporters instead of a few wealthy patrons simply writing larger checks. The Symphony Board and staff (and some musicians) embraced this challenge, identified 1,187 new or increased donors and secured over $600,000 the first year! Plus, a number of Board members not eligible for the match because of historical giving levels made three-year commitments while also increasing their giving.

The Symphony ended up raising over $800,000 in new dollars that first year in addition to our half-million-dollar match. Years two and three saw very little fall off in commitment payments, and other donors further increased their giving, enabling the Symphony to easily earn the $500,000 match every year.

To reiterate, anyone willing to provide support for three consecutive years is much more likely to get involved, attend more events (in this case performances) and become an advocate for the organization. One caveat to this example: Typically, it is not a good idea for a funder to initiate the structure of a challenge grant. The organization needs to own the strategy and have staff and Board members committed to it.

In this example, as Symphony fundraising progressed the first year, several clarifications had to be added to the challenge, such as gifts from a two-lawyer limited liability corporation being eligible alongside individual giving. I did not want the challenge to become focused on corporate giving instead of the intended goal of broadening individual support for the Orchestra. However, there is room to be flexible to meet the spirit of the grant. ♀

OVERARCHING STRATEGY

Broaden Support Base

ALL EXAMPLES AND ideas presented here have one recurring theme: Broaden the base to minimize reliance on a small group of historical supporters. One hundred supporters contributing $1,000 each year is much healthier than one donor providing $100,000.

It may be hard to believe, but having one or even a handful of significant donors can be detrimental to an organization. One supporter providing too much annual assistance may lead other potential contributors to conclude their help is not needed because surely that one funder would never let the organization fail. I have seen circumstances where one funder offers to underwrite 100% of an operation for several years. Without taking proactive steps to ensure the program will continue once that support ends, a catastrophic operating budget event may loom down the road. It is always appropriate to have a sense of urgency to expand the support base and continue to cultivate existing donors.

The ideas in this book demonstrate various approaches to reach potential donors and increase support. There is no one best way, and each organization must determine what strategy best fits its situation, Board and staff capability, potential donor audience, and offers a realistic chance of achieving their goal. Having a plan for sustainability and communicating it should be a core strategy in developing the message to expand program offerings and encourage new, promising funders. ♀

SCHOOLS CAN TEACH EVERYONE

Tanglewood Elementary

A LOCAL PUBLIC elementary school implemented one of the simplest but most effective fund-raising ideas I have seen. Tanglewood Elementary is in an upper-middle-class neighborhood close to Texas Christian University. Although Tanglewood is an exemplary public school, the children of many families in the neighborhood attend private schools.

A few years ago, yard signs started appearing that simply said W.A.C. In just a few weeks, these W.A.C. signs were showing up in the front yards of families with students at the school, families with kids in private schools, and even families with no children living at home.

Peer pressure can be a very good thing! Residents *had* to have a yard sign in the Tanglewood colors that confirmed they "Wrote A Check" to support the school. This approach, with slight modifications to the sign, continues to be an annual source of school revenue. ♀

SCHOOLS CAN TEACH EVERYONE

Fort Worth Zoological Association

THE FORT WORTH ZOO is one of the top-rated zoos in the country. The success can be attributed to a unique public/private partnership operated by the private nonprofit Fort Worth Zoological Association. The organization receives some operating support from the City of Fort Worth but all enhancements are privately funded.

Several years ago, the Fort Worth Zoological Association was in the middle of a $100 million capital campaign. In a meeting with the champion mover and shaker behind the campaign, we discussed the success she had with major donors but also the need for broader community support from individual contributors. I shared with her the positive results of Tanglewood's W.A.C. approach, and her response came fast: "We're going to do that, too!"

A few weeks later, purple and pink signs shaped liked flamingos appeared in the yards of major contributors with the tag "I Went Wild!"—the theme of the Zoo's campaign. Suddenly the Zoo started getting calls from residents wanting to know how they could get one of those flamingo signs in their yard! Unlike Tanglewood Elementary, which did not have a minimum donation, the Zoo did. Their yard sign campaign was extremely successful in helping secure several million dollars while promoting the Zoo's expansion. ♀

SCHOOLS CAN TEACH EVERYONE

Fort Worth Academy

FORT WORTH ACADEMY is a private K-8 school that instituted a very creative fundraising approach. The strategy did not require any outside participation but rather was designed to appeal to individual families within the school.

Just days before school started, Fort Worth Academy held an open house for parents to "meet your child's teacher." In each classroom, teachers had created a wish list of items they would like to enrich the learning environment, things like field trips, sets of flashcards, specific books and creative learning games.

Willing parents could select one or more items and donate the amount needed for purchase. This strategy proved very successful because parents could see the direct correlation of their gift with the enhancement their child would receive during the upcoming academic year.

I always encourage organizations to have a wish list. For small things, social media is a good way to raise awareness. For more significant items, a list of opportunities in various price ranges is more likely to resonate with certain donors and spark an interest. ♀

SCHOOLS CAN TEACH EVERYONE

Fort Worth Country Day

FORT WORTH COUNTRY Day is one of the city's premier private schools. A key component of a healthy private school is charitable support above and beyond tuition income. Like most schools, Country Day has an annual appeal, and at certain giving levels Keystone donors are recognized as a Builder, Contractor, Architect, Developer, Capstone, or Innovator Giver. These levels entitle supporters to window stickers and acknowledgment in the annual report.

Country Day has been quite successful over the years in raising the minimum amount required to remain at various levels. The entry Keystone Builder level that once was $1,000 has incrementally risen to $2,000. There is always some resistance to these increases, but overall the results have netted significant growth in annual giving.

This fundraising approach has led to a second (and brilliant) step that works well for this specific audience but is definitely not appropriate for everyone. Each year Fort Worth Country Day sends out a draft copy of its annual report. Families and other supporters have the opportunity to confirm the way they are recognized, such as Mr. and Mrs. _____, John and Charlotte _____ or Charlotte and John _____. The second benefit of the draft report is that individuals can see which category they will be listed in along with other donors. Not surprisingly, some make an additional contribution so they can advance to a higher recognition level. ♀

PEER PRESSURE WORKS

Rotary Club of Fort Worth

ROTARY CLUBS HAVE been a part of civic life for 100 years. In order to have a greater community, national or worldwide impact many, Rotary chapters have their own charitable activities that are handled through restricted funds such as an endowment or formation of a local foundation. The Downtown Fort Worth Rotary Club was, for a time, the third largest in the world. It supported the International Rotary Foundation as well as its own Rotary Children's Fund, a foundation focused on the needs of local children.

For years, during the meetings, Rotarians were encouraged to support these efforts, and eventually the appeal evolved into a (voluntary) line item on the dues statement. Support really took off when the Club took another step to recognize contributors. Members attending Rotary meetings wear an oversized blue and white badge with their name on it. But for members who made at least the minimum recommended semiannual contribution to the local philanthropy, their badge names became gold instead of white.

It was painfully evident at every meeting who was supporting the charitable activities and who was not. Each week more and more badges turned gold until it was rare to ever see a blue and white badge at a meeting!

This fundraising approach was simple and, even better, provided an ongoing source of charitable operating support as dues (and donations) continued to be collected semiannually. ♀

PEER PRESSURE WORKS

Jewel Charity Ball

FOR OVER SIXTY years the Jewel Charity Ball has raised money for Cook Children's Medical Center in Fort Worth. This event has contributed over $60 million to help cover uncompensated care.

Each year "Angels" make significant contributions, and a number of tickets also are sold for the opportunity to enter drawings for automobiles, trips, shopping sprees, one-of-a-kind experiences, etc. These tickets range from $10 to $100 and are sold during men's and ladies' events leading up to the gala where the winners are announced.

The night of the gala (and drawings), new, first-year members of Jewel Charity are still out in the crowd selling tickets. So, at this glamorous, black-tie gala featuring some seriously expensive jewelry being worn (it is, after all, the *Jewel* Charity Ball), as an incentive to purchase even more tickets, plastic rings and lapel pins with flashing lights are given away to those buying tickets that evening.

It is amazing to see hundreds of these inexpensive flashing lights being worn alongside gold and diamond jewelry, but it's a tangible sign of who is generously supporting the children's hospital. Peer pressure at its finest. ♀

CREATIVE CHALLENGES — DONOR BASE STRATEGY REVISITED

Presbyterian Night Shelter

ONE OF THE continuing challenges in fundraising is identifying new donors. One subset of that strategy must focus on maintaining historical supporters. The Presbyterian Night Shelter (PNS) was most successful with an appeal that targeted lapsed donors who had not given in the past three years.

The Foundation offered a match to incentivize giving during the summer months, which is typically a slower fundraising time. Before agreeing to this, we strongly encouraged PNS to be certain before mailing the appeal that their data base had been carefully reviewed. We insisted that all people receiving the mailing were known to still be living. A solicitation addressed to Mr. and Mrs. ____ when one of them was deceased would not garner a favorable response.

Lapsed donors should be easier to reconnect with because they had already at one time believed in the organization, as opposed to having to cultivate a first-time supporter. The offer to match gifts was effective in helping re-establish some relationships with past donors and generate recurring support. ♀

CREATIVE CHALLENGES — TARGETED MATCHES

United Community Centers

FOR OVER A century United Community Centers (UCC) has provided comprehensive social services to economically disadvantaged children, at-risk youth, unemployed and underemployed men and women, the elderly and families in crisis. The agency provides leadership in moving people from welfare to work and from dependence to independence.

A number of years ago, United Way restructured its funding strategy to allow donor designations. United Way had long acknowledged that UCC was very effective with the families they served and, as a result, provided significant annual operating support. Unfortunately, UCC had limited visibility in the community and lacked a strong donor base, which translated into a significant loss of United Way support once donor designation began.

During our meeting to address their operating budget issue, I encouraged UCC to return to their roots when it was established by local Methodist churches. Every Methodist church has a local missions budget, so a good place to start rebuilding a funding base would be reconnecting with the original source of support.

In this case, the Foundation structured its challenge grant around matching new or increased gifts not from individuals but from the local Methodist churches. Many ministers and lay leaders were unaware of the historical connection but responded generously to the matching opportunity. An important bonus was that Sunday School classes began getting involved with UCC, which led to more volunteers. As often is the case, once someone sees the impact an organization is having and the faces of those being lifted up, individual donations began to follow. ♀

CREATIVE CHALLENGES — MATCH DESIGNED TO CREATE A SENSE OF URGENCY

Child Protection Connection

THE ULTIMATE GRANTMAKING goal is to help organizations become self-sufficient so they no longer depend on annual fundraising. That scenario is unlikely, but I'm always looking for opportunities to help groups move in that direction.

In one instance we participated in a strategy to encourage *state* participation. The Child Protection Connection (CPC) is a niche organization that provides online resources to attorneys and judges handling child abuse and foster care issues. Often these cases are assigned to young, inexperienced attorneys or those with limited resources. Likewise, not all judges have experience dealing with the myriad of issues that must be considered in child custody court proceedings.

CPC provides a checklist of issues that must be addressed by the court as well as case law to support the positions. Texas attorneys and judges find this online resource incredibly useful, and it also allows them to communicate with other attorneys dealing with similar cases.

As a result of CPC national conference presentations, other states began expressing interest in this online resource. The Foundation's strategy was to provide CPC with an incentive matching grant to offer its services for half price to the first two states agreeing to sign a two-year contract.

It was my belief that once attorneys in another state had access to this resource, there was no way the state would take it away. In reality, the Child Protection Connection could only add two states in a twelve-month period, but emphasizing that the match was limited to two states did create a sense of urgency to take advantage of the discounted price, plus it created competition among interested states.

From a business plan perspective, once ten states were enrolled and operational, the entire enterprise would be self-supporting. Any additional states that signed on would not only benefit from the information available but would support further enhancements to the CPC's resource-providing capability. ♀

HELPING ORGANIZATIONS HELP THEMSELVES

Introduction

PERHAPS THE MOST strategic service a funder can provide is helping organizations find ways to support themselves. Executing this strategy requires a realistic business model and talented personnel with the proper skill set. It's interesting that some funders seem to discourage efforts toward self-sufficiency because that would mean nonprofits are unfairly competing against taxpaying organizations. But without program service revenue and earned income, nonprofits would be even more dependent on philanthropy and government support.

In my mind, if an organization, as a part of its mission, can assist others, it becomes not only more independent but able to expand its impact and, in many cases, provide employment or job training. The following examples offer a variety of approaches we have taken to help nonprofit organizations become more creative and self-reliant. ♀

HELPING ORGANIZATIONS HELP THEMSELVES

Catholic Charities
Fort Worth

WITH THE RIGHT leadership and business plan, some non-profits can provide services that become net cash generating enterprises.

Catholic Charities Fort Worth operates a number of human service programs. Many serve refugees and immigrants from around the world. It's not surprising that most of these individuals do not speak English, but they still must deal with social workers as well as legal, educational and healthcare systems.

All of these interactions require translators who must be paid. Catholic Charities realized they had existing relationships with many individuals who spoke these languages and many former clients who were now bilingual and had successfully assimilated into the United States.

Further, all of the organizations Catholic Charities partnered with needed reliable translators and were willing to pay for interpretation services. Catholic Charities worked with the Center for Nonprofit Management (now CNM) in Dallas to develop such a business plan. The Foundation provided first-year underwriting to hire a manager and launch the enterprise.

Within a couple of years, Catholic Charities Fort Worth was providing translation and interpretation services in over 100 languages. In addition to generating over $1 million in revenue, they could offer more services to more clients while at the same time providing good wages for many people able to speak English as well as those other languages.

Once Catholic Charities saw the potential of social enterprise, they began looking for other opportunities. The next shared revenue opportunity focused on underemployed immigrants who were adept at knitting. Catholic Charities contracted with colleges and universities to provide knitted scarves, gloves and caps in school colors. Again, this program brought net income to the agency and income for many immigrant women able to work from home. ♀

HELPING ORGANIZATIONS HELP THEMSELVES

Fort Worth Museum of Science and History

THE FORT WORTH Museum of Science and History has been a local mainstay for more than 75 years. Back in the 1980s it was an early adopter of the IMAX theatre technology, which provided significant net operating income for a number of years.

As a result of relationships around the country, the Museum had an opportunity to invest in a new digital IMAX film based on the technology that created the Soaring attraction at EPCOT in Walt Disney World. This film, *Flying Across America,* would provide content for the planned repurposing of the local IMAX theatre. Plus, by owning one-quarter of the new production, the Museum would be in a position to receive royalty income everywhere the movie was shown.

The Museum also created another royalty stream by developing a traveling exhibit based on *CSI,* the Crime Scene Investigation television show. A number of science and history museums around the country created a consortium to share content. The concept was each museum would develop one traveling exhibit that would premier locally, then travel to multiple museum venues around the country along with some type of ticket revenue sharing arrangement. ♀

HELPING ORGANIZATIONS HELP THEMSELVES

Texas Ballet Theatre

BALLET ORGANIZATIONS SPEND significant sums of money to either build sets or rent them from other companies. Several years ago, the Texas Ballet Theatre had the opportunity to purchase the sets and costumes for *Dracula* from a company going out of business. Always a popular offering around Halloween, *Dracula* is performed each year in locations around the country.

The Foundation helped fund the local ballet's acquisition of the *Dracula* costumes and sets, which it rents to other ballet companies in years they're not being used. In addition to not having any of the usual expenses when it performs *Dracula*, by renting these sets and costumes, the local ballet company receives additional revenue.

Based on the success of this rental model, the Foundation has since assisted the company in becoming co-owner of a storybook ballet based on *Pinocchio*. This is the first new storybook ballet in a long time, and if it proves to be popular, it will provide royalty income for years to come. Again, in addition to not having to pay rental royalties when they present it, each time another company performs the ballet, the Texas Ballet Theatre will receive income. ♀

HELPING ORGANIZATIONS HELP THEMSELVES

Metroport Meals on Wheels

METROPORT MEALS ON Wheels operates in northern Tarrant County. Their business model does not involve operating a commercial kitchen. Instead, they have established partnerships with several hotels and restaurants to provide an agreed upon number of meals each day.

Like a number of nonprofits, Metroport Meals on Wheels operates a thrift store to generate revenue. Unlike many organizations, much of the donated clothing is not appropriate for resale in a thrift environment. Being near several affluent suburbs, on a regular basis Metroport receives designer clothing and evening gowns, sometimes with price tags still attached.

With the Foundation's financial assistance, Metroport developed a business plan and opened a boutique thrift store. *Sadie's Upscale Consignment and Resale* was in a separate location where shoppers could schedule private appointments to view and try on clothing that had been set aside in advance. This retail operation has proven to be very popular both with shoppers looking for bargains and with donors knowing that expensive donated clothing was being resold for reasonable amounts with the money going toward the worthy cause of providing meals for the needy. ♀

HELPING ORGANIZATIONS HELP THEMSELVES

Presbyterian Night Shelter

THE PRESBYTERIAN NIGHT SHELTER (PNS) is one of the cornerstone organizations serving the homeless in Fort Worth. Through the years, PNS has grown from just a nighttime shelter for men to operating a separate women's shelter, another for women with children, and a separate facility for veterans. They also provide case management programs to assist with birth certificates, identification cards and health benefits.

PNS went a step further by creating an enterprise called Clean Slate (now Upspire) that provides employment opportunities and training. The first business endeavors focused on litter pickup, street median maintenance and janitorial services for office buildings and sporting event venues. After the pilot program proved successful, landscape services and other general employment staffing were added. All of these sectors address unmet community needs while providing job experience and income for PNS clients ready to return to the workforce.

Foundation start-up funding covered the initial supplies and uniforms necessary for PNS to fulfill these contracts with the City and private businesses. ♀

HELPING ORGANIZATIONS HELP THEMSELVES

Amplify

AMPLIFY PROVIDES VOCATIONAL opportunities for adults with developmental disabilities and has proven to be very successful at being more than just a sheltered work environment.

One of their most creative endeavors was offering document destruction and shredding to area businesses. With safety and security precautions in place, local government agencies and financial institutions were quick to sign on for the service, which includes collecting sensitive documents in secure containers along with same-day destruction. Workers with developmental disabilities who are in the shredding program feel a healthy sense of personal accomplishment while providing a valuable service.

Foundation funding expanded the inventory of rolling containers, which offer secure locked tops with only a slot to insert documents to be destroyed. Grants like this help establish or expand income streams and assist organizations in their ability to fulfill their mission. ♀

HELPING ORGANIZATIONS HELP THEMSELVES

Center for Transforming Lives

THE CENTER FOR Transforming Lives originally was the YWCA of Tarrant County. For decades they operated in a historically significant building that was once an Elks Lodge. In addition to the essential social services they provide, their prime downtown location featured a beautiful ballroom that was a popular venue for daytime meetings, wedding receptions and other evening events.

The Foundation tries to avoid funding general operating budgets because there's no easy exit strategy once annual support begins. In this case, the Foundation provided recurring maintenance support to enhance the ballroom so it could remain a desirable rental facility. Over the years we have provided funding to: refinish the floors; replace furniture and window treatments; upgrade lighting and audio/visual capability; and, more recently, update the kitchen to offer catering services, creating yet another revenue source.

In my mind, in addition to helping generate a revenue stream, by addressing specific maintenance items we were able to free up a portion of their budget to provide support for other essential parts of the operation. ♀

HELPING ORGANIZATIONS
HELP THEMSELVES

Helping Restore Ability

HELPING RESTORE ABILITY (HRA) provides attendant care for individuals who are paraplegic, quadriplegic or physically compromised at birth or due to injury. A significant portion of their revenue comes from state sources, which is both good and bad.

Texas law requires that HRA must accept all requests for management of care, for which the state will reimburse the agency. Reimbursement always has a lag time, which means the organization needs ample reserves to cover the vetting, hiring, training and paying of attendants until reimbursement begins. The Foundation has helped HRA meet this growing demand by helping create an operating reserve.

Another (nonrecurring) grant helped underwrite the cost of enhancing HRA's reporting capability to avoid any further delay in reimbursement due to errors in coding or billing. Software improvements eliminated the need for paper reporting and data entry, which limited the number of times information had to be entered into accounting, payroll and billing systems. These improvements streamlined staffing, reduced errors and meant faster receipt of state reimbursements.

Encouraged by these successes, the Foundation next helped HRA address tracking attendant hours of service. Hundreds of employees traveling to clients' homes create a challenge in confirming when attendants arrive and depart. The Foundation helped HRA install a tracking system in each client's home that was linked to mobile phones, enabling employees to enter a time-sensitive code when arriving and leaving. This proprietary system tied directly to payroll processing, which created a secure method for capturing hours worked. It saved HRA time and money, and became an asset that could be licensed to similar providers for a royalty fee. ♀

HELPING ORGANIZATIONS HELP THEMSELVES

Hillsdale College

HILLSDALE COLLEGE OFFERS public forums that communicate the fundamental principles of freedom on which Western civilization is based by exploring public policy issues and broadening the debate to include not only political and economic, but moral considerations. The Foundation helps underwrite these seminars, which are held in major cities throughout the country. Nationally and internationally known speakers explore the tenets of individual liberty, limited government, the free market and the Judeo-Christian heritage.

In addition to those who attend the National Leadership Speaker events in person, the seminar's impact is magnified through reprints of speaker remarks in *Imprimis*, Hillsdale's monthly speech digest, which in 2024 reached over 6.7 million subscriber/readers. For a small college with fewer than 1,500 students, Hillsdale has a huge audience who value the thought-provoking information received through *Imprimis* and online courses. Many individuals voluntarily choose to support the institution in appreciation of the valued content. ♀

INCENTIVIZE OTHERS TO GIVE

Hillsdale College

ANOTHER WAY THE Foundation supports Hillsdale College is by funding the Texas Scholars Program. As a way to attract exceptional students, we provided a pool of funds so Hillsdale can select one Texas resident as its Amon Carter Scholar (which includes a generous financial aid package). For another student from Texas each year, half of his or her tuition can be offset by being designated a Texas Scholar by the college.

We helped pioneer this scholarship model a number of years ago. The demonstrated success in recruiting and retaining highly qualified Texas students helped Hillsdale attract donors in other states to establish similar scholarships for outstanding students in their locale to consider the College. This type of support is vital since Hillsdale accepts no government aid. ♀

INCENTIVIZE OTHERS TO GIVE

Project HandUp

PROJECT HANDUP WAS the inspiration of former Burlington Northern Santa Fe Railway CEO Matt Rose and his wife, Lisa. They envisioned a community environment where women and children seeking a fresh start from an abusive relationship could have a place to live, a time to heal and prepare for a future independent successful life. The result was The Gatehouse in Grapevine, Texas, located on a secure 55-acre site, including four housing communities of 24 two- and three-bedroom apartments, a chapel, a general store, a training center and child care.

In addition to their personal investment in the project, Matt and Lisa championed a very successful capital campaign. Before they began, we discussed the big difference in raising one-time capital support compared to the real challenge of identifying ongoing operation and maintenance support. In response, Matt and Lisa again were personally generous in establishing an endowment to generate a revenue stream, but there remained a need for annual community assistance.

The Gatehouse has numerous volunteers assisting the professional staff and they have been successful in attracting individual donors to invest in adopting a family. For privacy and security reasons, the identity of individual families is not disclosed. In addition to helping with the capital campaign, the Foundation offered $10,000 as an incentive for every new donor willing to become a First Family Adopter at the $25,000 level. Within five years, The Gatehouse had secured underwriting sponsors for all 96 families!

The Gatehouse is a unique situation in many ways. It is a model of success in engaging a donor population with significant capacity to get and stay involved. This example is a reminder that incentive matches can be a good way to get others involved by making it easier to say "Yes!" the first time. From that point on, it's up to the individual entity to keep the donor engaged. ♀

SILENT MATCH

Overview

MANY TIMES, HAVING a foundation or well-known name willing to match first-time supporters, increased levels of support or all gifts can be an effective strategy. However, *not* having a prominent name may be more of an incentive where a donor is not comfortable thinking he or she must have someone's help to make a gift. In the following examples the Foundation wanted to give the fundraising organization flexibility in encouraging donors to get involved or increase their participation. ♀

SILENT MATCH

Jewel Charity

As HIGHLIGHTED EARLIER, Jewel Charity has raised millions of dollars to help Cook Children's Medical Center in Fort Worth, partially through offering flashing rings the night of the party for people buying gift drawing tickets. In addition to New Member, Men's events and Women's events throughout the year, significant contributions come from Angels who provide major gifts in advance of the annual Jewel Charity Ball.

As with all of these examples, the strategy works not because of the idea but as a result of the cause being supported and the creativity, personality and tenacity of the individuals involved. Jewel Charity has Angel levels ranging from $3,000 to $100,000. One year the Angel Committee focused on encouraging existing donors to increase their giving to higher recognition levels. The specific group targeted was historically giving $10,000–$15,000 with the goal being to move them to the $25,000 level.

The Foundation's grant gave the committee a pool of flexible dollars to negotiate with donors in this group to provide a silent match to supplement their increased commitment so they could reach the $25,000 category. The thinking (which was correct) was that once donors were recognized at this more prestigious level, they'd remain there in future years. The one-year silent match proved to be an effective lever in increasing ongoing support for Jewel Charity. ♀

SILENT MATCH

Junior Achievement of the Chisholm Trail

NOT ALL SILENT matches have to target individuals. To repeat, the goal is to broaden the support base and make it easier for contributors to say "Yes!"

Junior Achievement gives students a wonderful exposure to financial education. The JA model depends heavily on partnerships with local businesses to adopt a school and provide volunteers to teach the JA curriculum. Obviously, to grow the program and reach more schools JA needs a pipeline of new businesses willing to get involved.

At the time of our grant, corporations were being asked to commit volunteers plus $6,000 for materials and training. Our silent match pool of funds was available to help JA negotiate the required cash contribution in case a potential first-time partner agreed to provide volunteers but balked at the price. In most cases, once the corporation got involved with the adopted school, continued participation and funding at the full price point was not an issue. ♀

SILENT MATCH

Make-a-Wish Foundation North Texas

AFTER I SHARED the Junior Achievement example with Make-a-Wish Foundation North Texas, they requested support to implement a similar strategy to encourage first-time individuals, couples and groups to take ownership of granting an entire wish start to finish.

At the time of our grant, an average wish was around $7,500. The Foundation's silent pool of funds provided up to $2,500 to help new groups plan and execute a child's wish. Like many other examples, the experience and reward were so positive that once donors saw the impact, they wanted to do it again, even at a higher cost. ♀

SILENT MATCH

STAR Sponsorship Program

THE STAR SPONSORSHIP Program provides financial support for low-income families seeking to enroll their children in parochial and private schools. STAR recruits successful individuals to adopt promising students and pay a portion of their tuition as well as become a mentor and source of encouragement. Each student's family must apply to the program and financially participate in their child's education. STAR donors contribute $3,000–$5,000 in tuition assistance each year.

The Foundation annually provides STAR Sponsorship with funding to offer first-year donors the opportunity to get involved at a lower contribution level. Again, STAR Sponsorship donors all have significant resources. They do not need the help, but STAR uses our funding as an incentive for first-time, first-year donors to introduce them to the program. Once they see the impact their participation is having, future contributions at the full amount are not a problem.

Many of these donors continue their financial participation beyond the eighth-grade level (when STAR stops) and into high school, college and even graduate education. ♀

SILENT MATCH

The WARM Place

THE WARM PLACE (What About Remembering Me) provides group counseling and therapy for children who have lost a parent or sibling. Grief support groups have few earned income prospects and greatly depend on fundraising activities.

A major portion of The WARM Place operating budget comes from an annual gala. To help with fundraising, one year the Foundation agreed (silently) to match all two-year commitments, provided the donor would increase support the second year. For example, if a historical $2,500 donor agreed to support the current year's event but would also commit $5,000 for the following year, the Foundation would do a silent match of $2,500 so the donor would be recognized both this year and next at the $5,000 level.

In addition to increasing income for the current event, fundraising for the following year was already off to a great start! ♀

SILENT MATCH

Trinity Habitat for Humanity

ON A LARGER SCALE, the Foundation worked with Trinity Habitat for Humanity to establish a pool of funds to incentivize organizations to build their first house. At the time of this grant, the financial requirement to underwrite building a home was $50,000. The Foundation agreed to be the silent partner for first-time groups willing to contribute $25,000 along with the volunteer labor.

Many of the groups taking advantage of the match were churches. After a congregation built one house, the members insisted on doing it again. Just another example of whatever it takes to make it easier to get involved that first time.

On a non-fundraising note, one first-time construction team was composed of two accounting firms that were merging. Having a group building project in a neutral environment provided a unique team building exercise and gave employees from both organizations a chance to work alongside each other without titles. It turned out building a Habitat house as their first experience together solidified the decision to merge while creating an opportunity for people at all levels of the organization to bond. ♀

FINDING A WAY TO HELP

Community Storehouse

SOMETIMES THERE ARE organizations we want to help, but what they need is not a good fit for our funding policy. A long time ago we decided not to fund automobiles, vans, buses or trucks because once we started there'd be no way to stop or explain why we did it for one group but not another.

One organization that does a wonderful job in a large area under-served by nonprofits is the Community Storehouse. The Foundation had helped them several times with capacity building efforts, but one year their top priority was a new box truck. Community Storehouse operates a thriving resale store and the large geographic area it serves generates considerable donated furniture (which obviously brings a much higher price than most donated items). They had proof even more furniture was available if it could be picked up (in something other than an old truck that wouldn't leak oil on driveways!).

When Community Storehouse approached the Foundation, they asked us to make an exception to our no truck policy so they could continue to help themselves and not rely as much on us. I said I recognized the strategic need for a new truck, but I repeated that making even one exception would compromise us with numerous other organizations.

However, a funder who wants to help an organization can find a way. I suggested they use some of their reserves to purchase the truck, then request a grant to replenish their reserve account. With this approach, the Community Storehouse got the truck it needed (even sooner), we were able to help, and I did not need to report that we funded transportation. ♀

FINDING A WAY TO HELP

Center for Transforming Lives

ANOTHER CARTER FOUNDATION policy is we don't fund endowments. We recognize the need for permanent reserves and applaud organizations that succeed in securing grants to build permanent reserves. Since we operate exclusively on our endowment, we believe it is much easier to contribute $50,000 to an organization each year than to give $1 million and expect them to generate $50,000 in annual income. In this example, the YWCA of Fort Worth (now Center for Transforming Lives) had been offered a challenge grant to endow their homeless day care program.

When YWCA leadership approached me, their appeal was surely we could make an exception this one time to endow homeless day care. My response was the same—once we make one exception, we are compromised when the next unique situation comes along. But we believed in the mission and wanted to help, so I proposed an alternative option.

Each year the YWCA hosted a very successful fundraising luncheon called Women Who Care Share that supported their annual operating budget. I suggested that for one year only, everything raised at the luncheon should go toward the endowment match. Then the YWCA could make a grant request to the Foundation for that same amount of operating support.

Through this approach, good progress was made toward completing the endowment match, we provided funding so operations were not disrupted, and reliance on the luncheon for operating support could resume the following year. Plus, we could report providing operating support, not endowment funding. ♀

FINDING A WAY TO HELP

Child Study Center

THE CHILD STUDY Center is another wonderful, unique organization in Fort Worth. Started in 1962, it has helped thousands of children and families. They had also done a phenomenal job of developing a generous donor base but recognized the need to seize the opportunity to grow their endowment before some of these longtime supporters passed away.

We were approached during the campaign planning phase to see if the Foundation might participate in the endowment effort. For the sake of consistency, I again declined but did indicate a willingness to help.

The Child Study Center was confident some annual supporters would make significant gifts to the endowment. However, there was concern how that might impact the annual operating support received from these donors. In the end we offered to replace the operating support provided by donors who made an endowment gift equal to ten times their typical operating gift. Again, we found a way to help the Child Study Center grow its endowment by ensuring ongoing operations were not impacted. ♀

FINDING A WAY TO HELP

Southwest Christian School

SOUTHWEST CHRISTIAN SCHOOL is another one of the private schools in Fort Worth competing for students, faculty and facility funding. Every community has families who would prefer a faith-based environment for their children's education but may have reservations about the caliber of instruction. Parents want assurance their children will be prepared for success in whatever comes after school.

The Carter Foundation is seen as a resource for all private schools in the area, and the challenge is finding the right fit for funding. At the time of this example, Southwest Christian had an excellent curriculum and reputation but struggled to retain specialized teachers, especially in math and science. As a result, the upper grade classes did not have full enrollment.

The Foundation's grant was designed to supplement salaries to help attract and retain teachers where needed and promote the school's academics. If Southwest Christian could fill the openings in its high school classes, the additional tuition received for just a few students would more than offset the ongoing higher teacher salary cost after grant funding ended. ♀

FINDING A WAY TO HELP

Tarrant Area Food Bank

IN ADDITION TO the Foundation's policy to not fund transportation or endowments, we try to avoid providing significant undesignated operating support because organizations quickly become dependent on this annual funding stream. I'm not saying we do not provide annual operating support to some organizations, but I always try to have an explanation for my recommendations to the Board that says more than just these are good people doing good work and need our help.

Tarrant Area Food Bank leadership is well aware of our approach and has done an exemplary job of creating pilot programs and finding new approaches to deliver more food to those in need. Their annual strategy is to identify opportunities and request first-year pilot funding. Successful results can then be shared with other funders that might be hesitant to support an unproven idea.

Over the years we have helped the Tarrant Area Food Bank start its Backpack for Kids program for weekend food delivery; a food purchase program to supplement donated items; mobile pantries in church parking lots to reach unserved areas, followed by mobile pantries going to senior centers; and finally, mobile pantries going to outlying areas identified as food deserts. More recently, we helped pilot food pantries in elementary schools in challenging demographic areas. One outside-the-box year, the Food Bank was offered access to the United Parcel Service proprietary routing system to help plan daily truck routes for maximum fuel efficiency and safety by designing routes that made only right turns.

Again, we likely would help the Food Bank every year, but by understanding our interest in finding creative ways to help, we were able to provide support, let them try new ideas, and expand food delivery capability. ♀

FINDING A WAY TO HELP

St. Philip's School and Community Center

ST. PHILIP'S HAS become a tremendous success story in inner-city Dallas. To emphasize how challenging the situation was, St. Philip's had the only building permit issued in its zip code in the *decade* of the 1980s. Influential Dallas civic leaders got behind Terry Flowers' vision to transform this troubled area and make St. Philip's a shining star for education. As a result of some personal relationships, we were approached to provide scholarship support once the school started making progress.

Although only thirty miles from Fort Worth, Dallas is not a Carter Foundation priority area given all of the closer-to-home needs. In my opinion, it would have been easy to approve scholarship funding but difficult to find an exit strategy to end that type of support.

Instead, after meeting with the Head of School and some of their Board members, I suggested we fund a strategic master plan to help develop and prioritize growth steps for the campus and surrounding area. This approach enabled us to participate in a non-recurring need plus give St. Philip's a stronger case to take to Dallas funders and say a Fort Worth foundation provided support. Fast forward twenty-five years, and the School and surrounding community are thriving! ♀

NOW FOR SOMETHING DIFFERENT

Introduction

I KNOW FROM experience that most people do not read the preface or introduction to a book. So I want to repeat some of the things mentioned on the first pages. I attended a session called Thirty Ideas in Sixty Minutes. The concept was to share an idea that a funder had that was a little different. You may recall the Phoenix foundation that realized if a family did not have money to feed their family, they would not have resources to feed their pets, so that foundation funded a program to include pet food in the food bank delivery.

After hearing this example, I immediately thought that if the food pantry knew the size of the family and ages of the children, why not include books with the food delivery? The initial idea presented had nothing to do with literacy, but that's what came to my mind. These examples are "a bit different" but might inspire a non-related idea to another challenge. ♀

NOW FOR SOMETHING DIFFERENT

Cancer Care Services

As THE NAME indicates, Cancer Care Services is dedicated to providing financial, emotional and social support to low-income, under-served cancer patients and their families. Cancer Care works within a network of community agencies and medical suppliers to provide all types of treatment-related assistance. Financial support has been the primary need of the patients Cancer Care helps. At some point the effects of treatment prevent many cancer patients from working full time, thus resulting in loss of income and, potentially, health insurance.

For several years Foundation support centered on their efforts to provide financial assistance to help individuals continue insurance coverage and appropriate treatment. This Health Insurance Premium Program remains critical because uninsured patients are much less likely to receive the medical care, treatment and therapies to successfully combat the diagnosis. Plus, on a leverage basis, insurance premiums provide a multiple amount of compensated care.

I encouraged Cancer Care to share the results of this program with the oncology groups treating their clients because it is in the physician groups' best interest to have insured patients. ♀

NOW FOR SOMETHING DIFFERENT

Grapevine Relief and Community Exchange

GRAPEVINE RELIEF and Community Exchange is a faith-based social service agency providing food, clothing, financial assistance, healthcare and other necessities to struggling families. GRACE is one of the very few social service providers in Northeast Tarrant County. From its beginnings 30 years ago, the demand for GRACE services has grown along with the population explosion in this region of the county.

To meet the needs of and better serve its clientele, GRACE added a health clinic. Demand for care grew rapidly, but the organization struggled to recruit enough volunteer physicians and nurses to supplement their small staff. In an effort to incentivize participation, the Foundation offered to contribute $1,000 to GRACE for each doctor who volunteered and $500 for every nurse. The idea was once volunteers were on site and realized the difference they were making, it would be much easier to keep them contributing their services. After volunteering, many medical professionals commented this type of work is what first attracted them to the medical field. ♀

NOW FOR SOMETHING DIFFERENT

Dental Health Arlington

DENTAL HEALTH ARLINGTON has a mission to provide preventive and pain-relieving dental service to low-income residents and educate children about good oral hygiene.

DHA is operated primarily by volunteer dental professionals who provide exams, X-rays, cleanings, fillings, extractions and a small number of root canals, crowns and dentures. Two dentists staff the clinic two days a week, and a hygienist comes one day a week. Three dental assistants work with the staff and volunteer dentists. Each Friday a separate group of volunteer dentists staff the clinic. Local specialists also see DHA-referred patients in their private practice at no cost to the patient or the organization.

The Foundation provided grant funding for one complete operatory consisting of a new chair, service delivery system, chair-mounted exam light, X-ray machine, doctor and assistant stools, and other permanent tools needed to equip the station. This way, volunteer dentists could use equipment similar to what they had in their own practice. This replication of their private office configuration increased volunteer satisfaction and proved to be much more efficient than using antiquated contributed equipment. ♀

NOW FOR SOMETHING DIFFERENT

Project Access Tarrant County

AN INDEPENDENT STUDY revealed that one quarter of all adults in Tarrant County lacked health insurance. The need was particularly pronounced among those out of work, self-employed and individuals earning less than $25,000 annually. Even with the safety net of the county-run John Peter Smith Health System, many people fell through the cracks and turned to emergency departments for their care.

In response, the Tarrant County Medical Society took the lead in creating Project Access Tarrant County. This program is a collaborative community effort composed of a network of volunteer physicians, partnering hospitals, charitable clinics, and ancillary partners who provide compassionate care for uninsured patients.

Potential patients are referred for enrollment by physicians volunteering in the program, partnering charity health clinics and hospitals. All patients approved for Project Access are assigned a primary care physician. Enrollees also have access to specialists, laboratory work, ancillary procedures, care coordination, inpatient hospital care, and drug benefits.

With start-up funding from the Carter Foundation and others, Project Access began with a volunteer medical director and a paid staff consisting of an Executive Director, medical social worker, community care coordinator, and charitable clinic manager.

The program functions well, and a growing number of health care providers have committed to participate by agreeing to donate their services for a set number of patients each year. The challenge is finding available facilities for surgical procedures. Volunteers for all services associated with surgery are available but there is no place to operate. Project Access approached us with the innovative idea of leasing space from private surgical centers on Sundays when nothing was scheduled.

This Sunday surgery strategy is working and the program continues to expand. The most recent request to us is for assistance purchasing medical supplies associated with surgery. All personnel time is volunteered but the surgical center does incur a considerable cost in imaging supplies, disposable items, and products needed for follow-up care after surgery.

All in all, a wonderful example of a community coming together with talented individuals offering a variety of skill sets and resources to serve those less fortunate. ♀

NOW FOR SOMETHING DIFFERENT

Southwestern University

SOUTHWESTERN UNIVERSITY HAS been around 175 years, and individuals familiar with this Texas school recognize it as an exceptional undergraduate liberal arts college. However, those encountering the name for the first time often assume it is a regional public institution. Southwestern students, faculty, staff, trustees and alumni often find themselves having to explain the university's name, location and reputation.

School leadership asked the Foundation to be a neutral source of funding for a potentially controversial marketing research project to evaluate the effect the name Southwestern University had on recognition and visibility. Alumni and current students were asked if the school's name was an important part of their allegiance. Prospective students, parents and high school counselors were asked if the name was positive, negative or neutral in their search. Graduate school admissions counselors and corporate recruiters were asked if the name was an asset, liability or didn't matter when students are considered for admission or employment. Donors were asked what was Southwestern's recognition and perceived quality compared to peer institutions.

Rhodes College in Memphis went through a similar process and name change (ironically from Southwestern) thirty years ago, and that institution has flourished.

Funding from a neutral foundation with no opinion on the outcome helped ensure a more candid, comprehensive and unbiased evaluation. At the end of the day, the name stayed. ♀

NOW FOR SOMETHING DIFFERENT

Gladney Center for Adoption

THE GLADNEY CENTER for Adoption is the leading non-sectarian, domestic and international private adoption and maternity service agency in America. Since its founding in 1887, they have secured loving, permanent homes for well over 30,000 children.

Gladney is dedicated to maintaining programs that create bright futures through adoption by supporting young women experiencing unplanned pregnancy; enhancing each child's potential by placement in a permanent family; finding forever families for children from other countries; helping fulfill the dream of parenthood; offering all clients lifetime access to post-adoption assistance; and educating the public about adoption.

Gladney recognized that marketing/advertising/outreach was critical to their "option of adoption" message. In addition to historical marketing strategies, Gladney developed a research-driven, cutting-edge, nontraditional marketing campaign that built on their existing message.

The first step was to expand internet reach with professionally developed videos on YouTube, Facebook and the Gladney website capturing with real-life emotion and empathy the testimonials and experiences of current and former Gladney birth mothers.

The second step used birth-mother recruitment posters at nontraditional sites such as bus shelters, bus benches and mobile billboards to establish connections with young women facing an unplanned pregnancy.

The final step, which the Foundation helped under-write, created an additional set of videos that were carefully scripted but intentionally designed to look homemade with young women sitting in their bedrooms at home talking to the camera about the choices they faced and their decision to choose adoption. These videos were posted on sites not directly linked to Gladney but monitored by them. ♀

NOW FOR SOMETHING DIFFERENT

Young Women's Leadership Academy

THE YOUNG WOMEN's Leadership Academy was the first single-gender public school in Fort Worth. It was designed to offer girls a dynamic learning environment that encourages critical thinking, inspires confidence and nurtures both the intellectual and social development necessary to be successful in life.

The YWLA has created a culture of GEMS (Girls Excelling in Math and Science) where high school graduation is expected and college completion is the goal. With the vast majority of students being the first in their family to attend college, YWLA recognizes that it takes a network to support these girls all the way through college.

All graduating classes have achieved 100% acceptance to four-year colleges and universities, and most students are accepted to several institutions and receive generous scholarship packages. The best way to find the right higher education fit is for the student and a parent to visit their top one or two choices. For the past several years, the Foundation has provided YWLA with a pool of funds so that students and a family member can visit schools where the student has been accepted and offered a scholarship.

Students make the trips and tour while school is in session to affirm they can envision themselves in that living/learning environment. These visits result in greater buy-in, enthusiasm and confident support from families while their daughter is away studying and changing her life trajectory for the better.

On one occasion, YWLA called to apologize because the visit was a disaster and the student wanted nothing to do with that school. They were surprised my reaction to the news was so positive because that confirmed why the program was important—to improve the odds that the right choice would be made in deciding where students should continue their education. ♀

NOW FOR SOMETHING DIFFERENT

Fire Station Community Center

THE FIRE STATION Community Center is located in the heart of Fort Worth's Near Southside, in what originally was Fire Station #10 — when horses pulled the fire trucks and the back of the station had stalls and hay barns.

The building was refurbished in the 1990s to provide an anchor for neighborhood activities. In addition to helping restore the building, the Foundation was asked to help establish a "twig" library.

All cities have a main library, and many have outlying branch libraries as well. But not one was known to have a twig library where there were no permanent books. Instead residents could order books that were then delivered to the community center where they could be checked out and returned after reading.

This approach proved cost effective for the Fort Worth library system and brought books to an otherwise under-served area of the community.

I always liked the "twig" name, but now the space is just called a mini-library. ♀

CAPITAL CAMPAIGNS

Overview

FUNDRAISING IDEAS AND strategies come in many forms. The same is true for capital campaigns. There is not any one way that will always work in a major fundraising initiative, but several essential steps can help identify the best approach for a given situation.

There must be a case statement that communicates a compelling story to justify why the project makes sense and is needed. In addition to having a realistic construction budget, funders will want to see a defensible pro forma projection of what anticipated income and expenses will look like after completion.

Disclosure of the organization's financial situation—income, expenses, assets, liabilities, cash equivalents, restricted and unrestricted reserves, interim financing capability—all go into the evaluation of whether the entity can absorb a larger-scale operation. Another issue that must be addressed is the expected impact on operating contributions during the capital campaign.

Having an independent feasibility study will help identify additional questions and provide an assessment of the project's chance of success at the proposed fundraising level.

As campaign planning begins, many groups develop pyramids as a visual to show how many gifts at multiple giving levels will be needed to complete the campaign. I prefer breaking campaigns into buckets. All buckets will not be the same size, but having a number of smaller goals broken out by constituencies helps funders see where their gift will make a difference.

As an example, Key School had a capital campaign for a new location. After the Foundation's commitment was approved, I was asked why I felt so confident about this campaign. My response: 1) The School already owned the land that was a significant part of the goal; 2) The feasibility study confirmed that several historical donors combined would meet 50% of the goal; 3) One family with significant resources was very enthusiastic about the project and had promised a sizable gift; 4) Key Board members all had committed to the campaign; and 5) School families would only need to contribute less than $2 million to reach the goal and have a new state-of-the-art campus. ♀

CAPITAL CAMPAIGNS

Overview (Part 2) — Early, Middle, End

CAPITAL CAMPAIGNS NEED early support and leadership gifts to get started. It goes without saying that gifts of all sizes are important to reach a goal. But for funders with leadership capacity, a commitment on the front end should be at a level that represents a significant contribution for them to send the message that they believe this capital project is important.

From my experience, the more advance notice a funder has of a campaign, the more likely the opportunity for maximum participation. No outsider knows what other projects are competing for funding at any point in time. By providing as much lead time as possible, a funder can better manage the optimum time to make a commitment. In some instances, that will be early in the campaign; other times it might jump-start the middle portion and reinvigorate the effort; or it just might complete what's needed to reach the goal. To reinforce the value of feasibility studies, it is an effective way to get information about capital campaigns in front of prospects as early as possible.

Campaign planning should always identify candidates for early, middle and closing gifts. I sometimes worry that so much emphasis is placed on reaching funding milestones necessary to apply for closing grants that there is no strategy of who will fill the remaining gap. If groups plan to approach national or outside-the-community funders, I urge them to make contact early on to gauge interest and seek guidance but wait until they are nearing completion in their fundraising before applying. ♀

CAPITAL CAMPAIGN STRATEGY

Break into pieces—
Tarrant Area Food Bank

THE TARRANT AREA Food Bank is the leading provider of hunger relief in the western portion of North Texas. As a member of the Feeding America and Feeding Texas networks, TAFB serves as the regional clearinghouse and nexus of food distribution for a 13-county area covering 10,000 square miles.

TAFB had not had a broad-based capital campaign since its inception in the mid-1980s. They were quite effective fundraising for operations, but for capital improvement needs they relied on Board members or approached a few foundations for transportation purchases or to help expand refrigerated areas or freezer capacity.

The time finally came when TAFB was out of space in their existing footprint. With available property across the street, the determination was made to acquire the land and construct an administrative building, then convert the existing building completely into a warehouse and distribution center.

The entire project was estimated at $12 million. TAFB asked for my thoughts, and I said it was a very ambitious goal unless they had an angel I was unaware of willing to help. If the Carter Foundation gave a million dollars and a couple of other foundations did the same and several six-figure donors stepped up, that might get them halfway to $12 million, but where would the other $6 million come from?

Instead of completely disrupting their annual operating support and spending countless hours developing a full-scale capital campaign, I suggested TAFB break the project into two pieces and approach their historical friends with a $6 million goal to buy the land and build the administrative building.

At the same time, communicate that TAFB planned to come back in three years with another $6 million project to complete transformation of the existing building into additional storage, refrigeration and freezer space. (The original budget included a generous inflation factor.)

This strategy worked well, especially when an angel did appear in the form of an estate that had recently started a foundation focused on feeding the homeless and hungry! I believe all funders participated in both components of the project. This approach took a little longer (four years) but addressed the need and did not disrupt any operating support. ♀

CAPITAL CAMPAIGN STRATEGY

Break into pieces—Dream Park

DREAM PARK WAS designed to accommodate all children and be a place where a child with special needs could go down the same wavy slide as anyone else, hand in hand with an able-bodied sibling or friend. The vision was ambitious indeed:

- Ramping systems to each play element and transfer station
- Toddler swings and adaptive swings with high backs for children with limited muscle tone
- Stainless steel roller slides to enable children with cochlear implants to enjoy the experience of sliding (plastic slides short out hearing devices)
- Sensory-rich environments, including musical elements
- Play elements that promote parallel play, creating opportunities for children to be together
- Adequate shade structures for children with difficulty regulating their body temperature
- Interactive panels designed to foster cognitive development and imagination
- Handicapped-accessible parking, extra wide sidewalks and ADA-compliant pavilions and picnic tables
- Easy access to all structures for wheelchairs, walkers and individuals with limited mobility

Rachel Churchill and her sister-in-law, Corrie Churchill Watson, spearheaded this Fort Worth project after seeing a similar park in another state (which was especially interesting to me since neither of them had a child with special needs).

The City of Fort Worth was very receptive and approved a centralized location in a city park that would replace an existing playground. I suggested breaking the project into pieces. The initial $1.2 million phase would prepare the site, install a rubberized pour-in-place surface and fence the 57,000-square-foot area. While this work was underway, the City agreed to complete an adjacent parking lot.

Once the site was available as a safe place to play, it would be much easier to add individual elements and play structures as funding was received. Concept images were very compelling, and various groups and funders quickly came forward.

Attempting to raise the total project cost at the outset probably would have been a nonstarter, but securing the early funding to affirm the vision and create a user-friendly play area made the remaining balance much easier to raise piece by piece.

CAPITAL CAMPAIGN STRATEGY

Break into pieces—
The University of Texas at Austin

A UNIVERSITY OF TEXAS at Austin capital campaign is one project I had absolutely no role in, but it provides an example worth keeping in mind.

A number of years ago UT was the first institution I ever heard announce a $1 billion capital campaign. At the time, it was an almost unimaginable philanthropic goal. The University did not fixate on that number but rather ran a series of smaller campaigns for Athletics; Scholarships; Endowed Chairs; the Schools of Architecture, Business, Law, etc.

The subtotals when added together put the billion-dollar number back in play. The more "modest" $100 million goals seemed to be amounts where donors could see themselves having an impact in their areas of interest.

One other thought had never occurred to me before the UT campaign. Some funders have an internal discipline never to be more than a certain percentage of a campaign. If that number was, say, 10%, their maximum gift to a subtotal campaign might be limited to $10 million versus a potential $100 million gift if the stated goal was $1 billion. ♀

CAPITAL CAMPAIGN STRATEGY

Model Home—
ACH Child and Family Services

ALL CHURCH HOME (now ACH Child and Family Services) has been caring for vulnerable children in Tarrant County since 1915. Its programs and services are designed to intervene on behalf of these children and provide a continuum of services focused on maintaining family involvement while placing children in the most appropriate setting to meet their needs.

In 2004 ACH was planning a capital campaign to build three group homes along with an adjacent training, counseling and visitation building on a cul-de-sac on the edge of a neighborhood. After hearing their plans, I proposed the Carter Foundation fund construction of an initial model home so other donors could walk through and see how the home would function as a better living environment for the children. If any modifications were necessary, they could be incorporated into building plans for group homes two and three.

I'm pleased to say other donors reacted very positively once they saw the program in action. Funding for the remaining projects on the cul-de-sac was completed in a short time. Little did I know this fundraising success would encourage ACH to dream even bigger, which also provides additional inspirational examples for this book. ♀

CAPITAL CAMPAIGN STRATEGY

Model Center — United Community Centers

FOR NEARLY A century United Community Centers has been providing comprehensive social services to economically disadvantaged minority children, at-risk youth, unemployed and underemployed men and women, families in crisis, and the elderly.

UCC operated three community centers in parts of the city with few social service resources. All of the locations were undersized and in poor condition. Like many nonprofits, UCC had little capital campaign fundraising history. Raising $6.5 million (15 years ago) to rebuild and expand all three locations seemed like a daunting goal.

Although difficult to choose, I suggested UCC select one center to rebuild first and get it completed as soon as possible. This finished example could help demonstrate how a well-designed facility could better serve more families in an inviting and improved manner.

Fundraising for one location could be accomplished much quicker than for three. It also provided the flexibility to modify any aspects of the building to function even more efficiently in the second and third locations. The City of Fort Worth was so elated with the first model center that they approved funding for the entire cost of the second location. This municipal affirmation and financial participation further simplified fundraising for the final building. ♀

CAPITAL CAMPAIGN STRATEGY

Phase 1A participation in planning—Fort Worth Country Day

FORT WORTH HAS an unusually large number of outstanding private schools in the southwest quadrant of the city. This concentration creates considerable competition to attract students, faculty and funding.

In the early 2000s Fort Worth Country Day engaged a campus planning and consulting firm to evaluate facility needs. As expected, dreams for an ideal campus were quite ambitious and very expensive. Although no timeline was established for future construction, one consensus conclusion was that infrastructure improvements needed to happen soon, starting with roadways, parking and relocating the campus entrance.

Grant funding from the Carter Foundation was used to hire an engineering firm to evaluate anticipated traffic flow as a result of planned highway expansion and tollway construction on two sides of the campus. Timing of these studies proved to be critical. The owner and developer of real estate adjacent to the campus embraced the findings and agreed to donate twelve acres of land. With this additional property available for a new entrance, the City of Fort Worth coordinated roadway construction and traffic signal placement into the school's plans.

Since it was somewhat "our idea," the Foundation agreed to match dollar for dollar the road work and campus entrance. This thoughtful initial step has allowed continued implementation of the master plan in phases. ♀

CAPITAL CAMPAIGN STRATEGY

Phase 1A strategic participation— Trinity Valley School

TRINITY VALLEY SCHOOL (TVS), another premier private school, built an entire new campus after receiving a large parcel of land as a gift. The first twenty years after relocation were focused on continued improvements to the academic space and endowment. Only then did the Building and Grounds Committee turn attention to an athletic master plan with:

- Enhancements to the North Field, including a fieldhouse for field hockey, soccer and lacrosse; restrooms; concessions; equipment storage areas; a wind break; and a new parking lot for cars as well as staging areas for visiting team buses and vans

- Enhancement to the stadium area, including an elevated press box; expanded seating for home and visitor spectators; a third gymnasium; training room; locker rooms; strength training and cardio fitness; team rooms, tennis shop and hitting wall; and regulation long jump and pole vault runways and pits

- Enhancements to the South Fields, including a fieldhouse for baseball and softball; restrooms; concessions; storage; batting cages; bleacher seating; and dugouts

Fortunately, this type of ambitious project could easily be subdivided depending on the interest of individual donors. Since TVS knew the Foundation was always interested in seeing a menu of opportunities, I was shown this comprehensive athletic master plan and site map.

To the School's surprise, my interest focused on only one item—the parking lot. First of all, the Foundation had previously decided not to participate in athletic facility projects for private schools. Our rationale was not a reflection regarding the importance of these endeavors but more a matter of there being no way to determine which ones, and at what level, were worth our investment.

However, this parking lot was another matter. In my opinion, none of their plans could move forward without major disruption until a new parking area was completed. Existing parking would be unavailable during some construction projects, and there had to be a safe place for student parking and for visiting teams to load and unload from vehicles. Further, having the parking lot completed made plans for North Field enhancements more compelling because prospective donors could see where their investment would go adjacent to this new parking area. ♀

CAPITAL CAMPAIGN STRATEGY

Preliminary funding to confirm location — Catholic Charities Fort Worth

IN 2005 CATHOLIC CHARITIES Fort Worth operated 24 unique programs serving 74,000 individuals. To comprehend the magnitude of that statistic: One out of every twenty Tarrant County residents benefited from at least one of its services.

Due to extraordinary growth in demand, Catholic Charities began evaluating its programs, facilities and plans. A new building site was identified, but there was some question if clients would go to a different location. Since campaign fundraising was just beginning, I suggested Catholic Charities rent space in a building across the street from the potential location and begin offering some services there to determine the response.

It was not long before demand for services at the new location dwarfed activity at the existing building. This experience confirmed that the new building site would be well received by the people being served (as well as the staff).

Results from the upfront grant support for the pilot location removed any remaining hesitancy in the minds of other funders that this is where Catholic Charities needed to be, and it continues to be true today. ♀

CAPITAL CAMPAIGN STRATEGY

Encourage others to do more—
ACH Child and Family Services

You RECALL THE ACH Child and Family Services model home example. A few years after that capital campaign, ACH received an offer they could not refuse to sell their main campus. Fortunately, ACH identified a large Masonic Home property that was ideal for their programming with plenty of room for expansion.

ACH launched another capital campaign to begin renovating existing buildings along with plans for new construction. The Carter Foundation was an enthusiastic supporter, but our commitment came with a twist. Instead of using our funds for one project, we gave permission to leverage our grant to encourage others to do more and receive an even higher naming recognition.

As an example, a $1 million naming opportunity was available for a remodeled building. A prospective donor might indicate interest in making a $500,000 gift. ACH had the ability to offer the scenario that if the donor could stretch to $750,000, an unnamed contributor (Carter Foundation) would silently contribute the remaining $250,000 in order for them to reach the million-dollar naming level.

This silent partner approach enabled ACH to incentivize a number of families to make the largest gifts they had ever made and receive recognition at levels they never imagined. Most of those donors have continued to be significant supporters due to the organization's work and their pride in being recognized on the campus. ♀

CAPITAL CAMPAIGN STRATEGY

Philosophy on recognition

RECOGNITION IS VERY important to some donors. There are others who might give even more with the promise *not* to publicize their gift. At the Carter Foundation, we know our name and participation often are crucial in getting campaigns off the ground.

With few exceptions, we do not "reserve" specific naming opportunities. I prefer organizations have as many options as possible to offer other donors. Organizations have never failed to recognize us in some meaningful way, and I always hope our participation helped them find as many additional donors as possible to acknowledge.

Here's one more caveat when a name is on a building. There will come a day when that building will look tired and need to be updated. The name on the building will be the first ask!

Final note. I understand some universities are starting to put time limitations on naming gifts so that buildings can be resold or renamed in ten or twenty years when updating or a change in function is needed. ♀

CAPITAL CAMPAIGN STRATEGY

Incentivizing others to get off the sidelines

NO MATTER THE size of a capital campaign, the last dollars always seem the most difficult to secure. In some instances, donors may hope someone else will meet the need and they'll be off the hook. In most situations it's probably more of a timing issue and the prospect might feel overextended and uncomfortable making the commitment being sought.

On several occasions I have advised organizations to let uncommitted prospects know that on a specific date, donor names will be permanently carved on the recognition wall. This incentive seems to be most effective with large gifts, but the definition of large varies case by case.

I further encourage organizations to work with uncommitted donors on a funding timetable that is mutually agreeable, but the signed commitment must be in hand before the drop-dead date for inclusion on the donor wall. ♀

CAPITAL CAMPAIGN STRATEGY

Matching grant philosophy

THE CARTER FOUNDATION has participated in numerous types of matching grants, many of which are noted in this book. We try not to have more than one challenge ongoing at any one time so as to not be viewed in the community as Matches"R"Us because that could dilute the impact the incentive match might have.

Most of our matching gifts are intended to broaden the funding base and hopefully provide continuing support in future years. Capital campaign matching gifts generally require a different strategy because they're designed to motivate a donor to participate in a way they might not otherwise consider. Also, donors with limited resources may not see how their small gift will make a difference in a multimillion-dollar campaign.

The following examples are an effort to dispel that misconception. ♀

CAPITAL CAMPAIGN STRATEGY

Bringing others along—
All Saints Episcopal School

ALL SAINTS EPISCOPAL School, another outstanding provider of private education in Fort Worth, started in a church as a kindergarten through eighth grade option. Enrollment growth prompted the purchase of a large tract of land and construction of new Lower and Middle School facilities.

This new learning environment led to demand for an Upper School, which resulted in the launch of an ambitious (for the time) capital campaign. Several generous families stepped forward with significant gifts, but they were not even close to what was needed. The next tier of prospects seemed hesitant to commit to a project with no clear path to completion.

Volunteer campaign leaders were all fully invested in the project when we met to discuss next steps. During the visit it came to light that nearly half of the families attending the school had enrolled their children since the move to the new location and had never participated in a capital campaign.

Fast forward, the Carter Foundation agreed to match gifts up to $25,000 from families who had not participated in any previous campaign. The hope was this incentive would encourage more generous giving. The challenge proved so successful that I had to go back to the Board for additional matching funds.

Two additional outcomes tied to this example. Another family in the school provided a parallel match for all first-time gifts of *more than $25,000*! And, after campaign pledges were fulfilled, annual giving participation rose to record levels as families continued to support *their* school. ♀

CAPITAL CAMPAIGN STRATEGY

*Bringing others along
(unicorn ending)—
Trinity Christian Academy*

TRINITY CHRISTIAN ACADEMY (TCA) is yet another private school just west of the Fort Worth/Tarrant County line that provides a quality education at a tuition affordable for most working families.

I had multiple visits with the school's leadership and followed their enrollment growth and expansion plans for a new secondary school building and gymnasium. Like many private Christian school capital campaigns, a small number of families had provided a significant percentage of the total giving.

TCA knew of the matching challenge the Foundation provided All Saints Episcopal and was requesting a similar arrangement. I always tell private schools that I recognize the majority of their families are already making a sacrifice just to be there. However, I also point out that the families who came before them also made sacrifices and that is why it was important for all families to be part of current building efforts.

In this case the Foundation was asked to match all gifts up to $1,500 with the hope every family would contribute at least $100. Well, they did. The balance needed to complete the project was not raised, but every family did participate.

This is where the unicorn comes in. The Weatherford newspaper wanted to run a story about Trinity Christian and the construction project. I had nothing to do with what happened next other than answer some questions via email about the project and why the Foundation chose to participate. I highlighted not only the 100% participation but the school's commitment to have every older student mentor a younger student.

A husband and wife in Weatherford with no relationship to the school read the article and called TCA. They said they drove by the school every day and always wondered what was going on with the construction project, and they asked if they could make a visit. You bet they could! They came out, looked around and asked, "How much do you still need to raise?" The school's answer was right at $1 million. They responded, "We believe we can take care of that right now!"

They went on to say they valued the school's mission and really liked the 100% buy-in participation. I still do not know who they are, but I understand they have continued to support the school by providing scholarships for children needing assistance to attend. ♀

CAPITAL CAMPAIGN STRATEGY

Broaden participation and create a feeling of ownership and belonging— Performing Arts Fort Worth

PERFORMING ARTS FORT Worth was established to raise funds to construct and operate the Nancy Lee and Perry R. Bass Performance Hall. Ed Bass spearheaded fundraising for the world-class Bass Hall, and it has become a pillar of the performing arts community and all of North Texas. Since its opening in 1998, millions of patrons have attended performances featuring the symphony, ballet, opera, Van Cliburn competitions, Broadway shows and popular artist concerts.

Mr. Bass personally secured tens of millions of dollars in contributions for the project. The Carter Foundation was a prospect for one of Ed's seven-figure asks. My predecessor at the Foundation, Bob Crow, expressed enthusiasm for the vision but suggested a different role for the Foundation to play. He encouraged Ed to continue his very effective fundraising efforts with large donors. After that phase was completed, then Ed could announce a Carter Foundation challenge match for all smaller gifts to encourage community participation.

The intent was to ensure Bass Hall belonged to the broadest number of people and not be just an edifice for the wealthy. The approach proved very successful, with thousands of donors participating and taking advantage of the opportunity to sign the permanent donor registry alongside those making larger gifts.

To re-emphasize how Bass Hall's is intended for all citizens, the Performing Arts Fort Worth Children's Education Program at Bass Hall has the goal each year for every
school-aged child to attend at least one age-appropriate
daytime concert given by the various performing arts groups
in town. ♀

CAPITAL CAMPAIGN STRATEGY

10% solution for Phase Two completion—Performing Arts Fort Worth/Maddox-Muse Center

BASS HALL USHERED in a new era in Fort Worth cultural life and quickly became a dynamic, vibrant force in the community. The need for the always-planned Phase Two came sooner than anticipated.

Across the street was the Maddox-Muse Center, envisioned to serve as a complementary facility featuring a Recital Hall, Rehearsal Hall and Atrium Lobby for receptions, lectures and pre-performance functions. The Recital Hall was designed with 40-foot ceilings capable of duplicating the acoustics in the Performance Hall. Plans for the Rehearsal Hall included 18-foot ceilings and a sprung floor for dance recitals, intimate musical performances and social occasions. Other areas involved renovations to create administrative space for the symphony and Performing Arts Fort Worth.

Virtually every significant donor to Bass Hall understood the need for this addition and appreciated the thoughtful planning that had taken place to design comprehensive, adjacent space. This situation spawned a most unique capital campaign appeal: If every major donor would commit 10% of what they had given to Bass Hall, Phase Two and the Maddox-Muse Center would be fully funded. It worked! ♀

CAPITAL CAMPAIGN STRATEGY

Early and late— Alliance for Children

Fundraising for capital campaigns needs to be flexible to accommodate interested parties' circumstances and limitations. The Carter Foundation's policy is not to encumber future-year grant budgets unless absolutely necessary. Approved capital campaign commitments must come out of the current year's grant budget regardless of when the payment will actually be made. As a result, we always report grants payable at year end, but funding is set aside during the year of approval. This discipline sometimes requires us to consider participation both at the beginning and near the end.

As an example, Alliance for Children (AFC) serves Tarrant County children suspected of being victims of abuse. The agency has locations in Fort Worth, Arlington and Hurst, and it works in partnership with Cook Children's Medical Center, the Tarrant County District Attorney's Office, the Sheriff's Department, the Department of Family and Protective Services, and fifteen municipal law enforcement agencies. Office space is provided on site for all partners because close communication and case management expedite results on behalf of the children.

With this large number of partners, it was easy to see why additional space was needed in all locations. AFC's campaign was another situation where there would be three building projects and some donors likely would support the location closest to their personal interests.

As a longtime AFC supporter, the Foundation wanted to be a lead contributor but was constrained in the amount available due to other competing projects at the time. We went ahead and committed all we could on the front end and gave the (non-binding) assurance that we would provide a second gift later to help complete the campaign. This second gift also provided a big help in completing another Foundation challenge grant at the end. ♀

CAPITAL CAMPAIGN STRATEGY

Everybody has a role—
Texas Christian University

EVERY CAPITAL CAMPAIGN is unique. No single playbook strategy can be duplicated from one project to another. However, completion roadmaps can help donors understand their role in a successful campaign.

Amon G. Carter Stadium on the TCU campus and the Amon Carter Museum of American Art and are two of Mr. Carter's best-known legacies. He believed a strong, nationally prominent university was vital to the success and healthy growth of Fort Worth. In the late 2000s TCU's academic and athletic reputations were on the rise and the campus was undergoing a phenomenal transformation along with record-high applications for admission.

But the football stadium had been built in 1930, and an upper deck and press box were added in the 1950s. That was it for upgrades. After fifty-plus years, obvious issues needed to be addressed.

The first step was the stand-alone South End Zone Project. The Foundation's interest and lead gift helped pay for new construction that added dining facilities, club seats and several suites so donors could experience how premium seating in a potential new stadium would look and feel.

Positive response to the South End Zone Project led to a Stadium Renovation Committee exploring numerous options. It quickly became evident that too many limitations existed to accommodate ADA issues of width, depth and height of rows, seats and steps; restrooms; and restricted movement through undersized portals.

Demolishing the stadium was never considered because of logistics, cost and length of time. The best solution would be to leave everything below ground level alone. The playing field would remain unchanged, and there simply would be modifications to the rake angle in the lower seating bowl. Construction would begin on the west side with improvements to north end zone seating and east side stands to come later.

The cost of first phase funding for just one side of the stadium seemed prohibitive until a plan was articulated for this to become a reality. The Carter Foundation would make the first commitment of $15 million. As expected, five other donors followed with similar Founder gifts. The remaining balance would come from sales of suites and premium club seating (which sold out in no time). This response level generated enough revenue to complete reconstruction of the rest of the stadium. Due to continued growth in demand for premium seating, another club level with more suites was later added on the east side.

Along with the football team's success, this investment in facilities played a critical role in TCU's invitation to join the Big XII Conference. Since the Foundation cannot receive any benefits for gifts, the Amon Carter Founder's Suite was given to the Chancellor to entertain guests during games in order to continue raising funds and promoting the institution.

As a footnote, I was enthusiastic about the Stadium project but concerned about the effect it would have on our philanthropy in the community. I never wanted to say I was sorry we could not help with an important capital project because we were building a football stadium. To compensate, I recommended we increase our payout ratio by one half of one percent to fund the Stadium and not impact the community. ♀

CAPITAL CAMPAIGN STRATEGY

Fallback plan and partnering— James L. West Center for Dementia Care

For years the James L. West Alzheimer's Center (later renamed Center for Dementia Care) was the only nonprofit, long-term residential, respite and day program in Fort Worth fully licensed to serve individuals with Alzheimer's disease and related dementia. When constructed twenty years earlier, the layout was state of the art but institutional, with large nurse stations and medical components throughout. Over time, newer facilities began emphasizing freedom, independence, normality, family involvement and meaningful activity in a setting that looked and felt more like home.

The West Center's capital campaign to remodel resident space easily could be broken into phases because each of the three floors consisted of two self-contained units. As construction progressed, each half floor could be vacated and residents relocated to other wings in the building. The results were phenomenal, but costs continued to increase for completion of each phase.

While patient census for the five available units remained full throughout the remodel, campaign funds were exhausted with still half of one floor to go. Then a fallback plan and ideal partnership emerged. Community Hospice of Texas (now Community Healthcare) provided end-of-life care for many of the West Center residents, and an agreement was reached to convert the remaining half floor into a hospice unit.

After hospice modifications and improvements were completed, residents and families did not have to move to another location and other hospice patients could be accommodated, which ensured all beds remained utilized. ♀

CAPITAL CAMPAIGN STRATEGY

Peripheral projects—
Texas Christian University

TEXAS CHRISTIAN UNIVERSITY was wrapping up funding for a new building. Due to other commitments on campus, the Foundation was not a candidate to be a significant donor. Rather than provide token support, we looked at campus needs surrounding the construction site.

Robert Carr Chapel is adjacent to the new building and a very popular venue for weddings and receptions. This corner basically functions as another "front door" to the University and is sometimes the only part of the campus visitors ever see.

Our participation was not a typical capital grant to TCU but was sufficient to fund enhancements and beautification for the parking lots and common areas around the new and existing buildings. ♀

CAPITAL CAMPAIGN STRATEGY

Peripheral projects—
University of North Texas
Health Science Center

THE UNIVERSITY OF North Texas Health Science Center (UNTHSC) is one of the nation's distinguished graduate academic institutions dedicated to education, research and public service. The 33-acre campus is home to:

- Texas College of Osteopathic Medicine
- School of Nursing
- School of Pharmacy
- School of Public Health
- School of Health Professions, including
- Physician Assistant Studies and Physical Therapy
- Graduate School of Biomedical Sciences

The campus has a wonderful location in the heart of Fort Worth adjacent to Fort Worth's world-class Cultural District. UNTHSC sits literally across the street from the Amon Carter Museum of American Art, Kimbell Art Museum and Fort Worth Museum of Modern Art.

UNTHSC made a concerted effort to include nearby neighborhood and Cultural District representatives in the planning process for continued growth and facility construction. State funding for capital projects covered most of the building costs, but the community thought the budget for the Public Health Education Building exterior design was inadequate.

To ensure the façade was aesthetically complementary, private funding was enlisted to add Texas Quarries Cordova Shell limestone to the building's lower portion for warmth, texture and character. ♀

CAPITAL CAMPAIGN STRATEGY

Incentivize other types of funding partners— JPS Health Network

JOHN PETER SMITH Hospital and the JPS Health Network are committed to providing accessible public healthcare in Tarrant County for residents who need it most. One of their most effective growth areas has been school-based health centers that serve as primary access points for well-child visits, vaccinations and treating minor ailments.

JPS and school districts jointly fund these health centers. School districts typically pay for the initial cost of the facility or renovations necessary to convert existing space. The district also is responsible for building operations and maintenance of plumbing, electrical and technology. JPS provides all medical equipment, furniture, supplies and staff salaries and benefits.

At the time of this example, Lake Worth ISD had an enrollment of 2,800 students and Castleberry ISD served 3,500 students. These districts are adjacent and both have modest tax bases and serve primarily low-income constituents.

Historically, Lake Worth ISD and Castleberry ISD competed with the much larger Fort Worth ISD for programs and funding. After JPS introduced the prospect of incentive funding from the Carter Foundation, the two districts agreed to partner and co-fund a central location where students and families from both areas could access high-quality healthcare at a low cost.

JPS could not afford two new locations, and neither district had the facilities or resources to do something on their own. This incentive funding went a long way toward finding a solution to improve access to affordable healthcare in Northwest Tarrant County. ♀

CAPITAL CAMPAIGN STRATEGY

Bring natural partners together—Arlington ISD and Boys and Girls Clubs of Arlington

THE BOYS AND Girls Clubs organization is recognized as one of the most efficient and effective youth development groups in the nation due to its ability to reach those in greatest need and offer the highest level of service.

Their mission remains to inspire and enable all young people, especially those from disadvantaged circumstances, to realize their full potential as productive, responsible citizens. This goal is accomplished by providing a safe place to learn and grow; ongoing relationships with caring, adult professionals; life-enhancing programs and character development; and the chance to experience hope and opportunity.

The Boys and Girls Clubs of Arlington (now part of Tarrant County) piloted a new concept by integrating a club location into a new Arlington ISD elementary school. In a first-of-its-kind partnership, the school was designed in the shape of a block C (i.e. ⊂) with the open part of the C configured for the Club to serve elementary school children and teenagers in several separate learning centers.

With this design, the Club had its own secure entrance on the side of the building along with adequate parking and outside play areas on the school property. Other features for after-school use took advantage of adjacency to the school cafeteria on one side, the gymnasium on another, and computer labs and restrooms on the remaining side.

This co-location was collaborative, creative and cost effective, and should be considered an option in future school construction. We were one of several funders that agreed to help with build out of the Boys and Girls Club space. I recognize some donors might hesitate to help fund a public school building, but most should be willing to help furnish, equip and operate a Club location. ♀

CAPITAL CAMPAIGN STRATEGY

Support from funders outside the local area

MOST FUNDING SOURCES concentrate on local projects where they have the most knowledge and believe they can have the greatest impact. Thankfully, some foundations have a state-wide or even national focus.

Whether a nonprofit is responding to a national request for proposal or seeking support from an out-of-area funder with a known interest in a specific topic, there should always be local support for the initiative already in place. Generally, there's no reason why someone far removed should care about a project if local community members have not already demonstrated their support.

In my opinion, if an organization can secure funding from a national organization, local participation should be required to earn the outside support. Local supporters should not want to "leave other money on the table" by not fulfilling any outside matching requirements.

A separate strategy to help secure long-distance support may arise when it can be demonstrated that residents from the funder's region are being served. This strategy might take the form of a school soliciting scholarship support for students from an area or by providing census data showing families from the funder's region are receiving specialized healthcare in the requesting organization's locale. ♀

CAPTAL CAMPAIGN STRATEGY

Prove yourself before trying to have a capital campaign— Recovery Resource Council

MANY ORGANIZATIONS ARE anxious to have their own building. Regardless of the size of the existing budget, capital campaign fundraising is always a challenge because it will be a multiple of the amount that must be secured in addition to ongoing operating support.

Most nonprofits start in space offered free of charge or with modest rent. As program delivery grows along with awareness, typically the desire grows to move to a larger space or add a second location.

Only after these growth steps have successfully been demonstrated can consideration of permanent space begin. One question seldom answered is how long will the planned building provide adequate space? I have seen situations where by the time fundraising was completed and the building was finished, it had already been outgrown.

Prospects for a successful campaign greatly improve when the need has been demonstrated and there's confidence in the leadership. This faith must include ability to raise the funds needed for the campaign, operate on a larger scale, and continue to generate sufficient revenue.

A number of years ago, the Recovery Resource Council had to find a new home because highway expansion was taking their rented location. At the time, the agency was not in a financial position to launch a capital campaign, but it did find an appropriate building to lease, and the building had a purchase option. This arrangement enabled them to demonstrate growth in services and justify the need for the larger space.

In setting an achievable campaign goal, part of Recovery Resource's strategy was to show how monthly rental payments could go toward debt service. Further, having the building in the nonprofit's name eliminated property taxes, further lowering future operating costs. ♀

CAPITAL CAMPAIGN STRATEGY

Helping them help themselves—
Community Enrichment Center

THE COMMUNITY ENRICHMENT Center operates several programs designed to break the cycle of hunger, homelessness and poverty in Tarrant County. One impactful program, the Adopt a Family Partnership, provides transitional housing for homeless families.

An extension of Adopt a Family was an initiative to provide a secure housing environment for women and children escaping domestic violence. This vision led to the purchase of a gated apartment complex that was internally named Open Arms Home.

The Foundation was approached to help refurbish and renovate some of the units into larger configurations for mothers with several children. Since I was new in my role at the time, I was trying to understand how the Community Enrichment Center could afford to buy and operate an apartment complex along with its other housing programs.

I discovered that in addition to generous support from several churches, the organization operated an extraordinarily successful resale shop. I was told it was so popular that the shop staff and volunteers could hardly process all the donations. I asked if opening a second resale shop location had been considered. The response was yes, but all efforts were focused on getting the Open Arms Home ready for occupancy.

I told their leadership that I had more interest in helping them help themselves by establishing a second resale location.

The Community Enrichment Center happened to have a Board member in the real estate business who scouted locations for a national retailer. He identified an ideal location and the Foundation provided several months of start-up funding. Soon the new store was generating monthly net income equal to our grant. This revenue stream provided ongoing support for the Open Arms Home refurbishment and monthly operations. ♀

CAPITAL CAMPAIGN STRATEGY

Helping others after they prove themselves — Trinity Habitat for Humanity

EARLIER I SHARED how the Foundation was a silent partner with Trinity Habitat for Humanity in encouraging groups to build their first home. As years went by, additional opportunities to support the organization arose.

To further help Trinity Habitat support itself, we responded to a request to establish a pilot Re-Store location (which subsequently led to several others) where do-it-yourselfers and rental property owners could buy surplus windows, bricks, plumbing, hardware, tile, etc. Once the Re-Store was established, many local contractors began donating excess materials, which led to even greater revenue to support Habitat.

Later we were approached to participate in funding a property purchase pool to implement Habitat's vision to not acquire one lot at a time but rather secure contiguous lots and blocks in neighborhoods to accelerate change.

Most recently, we were asked to assist with infrastructure installation for an entire subdivision. Habitat was able to purchase acres of property on the outskirts of Fort Worth for what it had been spending to acquire individual lots. We never would have approved our seven-figure gift without Habitat's record of success with previous smaller initiatives. ♀

PHILOSOPHY ON ENDOWMENTS

Introduction

ENDOWMENTS PLAY A critical role in providing financial security and sustainable support. I would not have these examples to share if the Amon G. Carter Foundation had not been established as an endowment.

Endowments require realistic investment guidelines, financial discipline, conservative spending policies and independent governance. I often say it is much easier to give an organization $50,000 each year than provide $1 million and expect them to annually generate $50,000. I know how we manage our assets, but that does not mean a nonprofit can replicate those results.

Another factor is leadership over time. Donors may have all the confidence in the world in the current CEO and Board, but there's no guarantee that future leadership will deliver the same level of management and operating results. One guardrail is to have endowment assets professionally managed in a separate entity tied to the nonprofit or by a bank trust department or community foundation. Having an independent fiduciary should provide some assurance for continuity in spending policies and financial discipline.

Another issue to consider is what happens to the endowment if the nonprofit goes out of business or changes its mission or services. More established organizations such as educational institutions or hospitals have a size advantage and enjoy a higher level of confidence there will be perpetual operations compared to a smaller, narrowly focused entity.

The more time passes between the establishment of an endowment and the original founders'/funders' involvement, the greater the chance for change or drift in mission, values or focus. For these reasons, the Carter Foundation does not directly fund endowments. However, we do want to help organizations achieve their endowment goals. The following three examples are strategies the Foundation has used to do just that. ♀

ENDOWMENT FUNDING STRATEGY

Parallel participation—YWCA
(previously mentioned but worth repeating)

FOUNDATIONS (AND OTHER donors) consider a variety of funding opportunities along with heartfelt, emotional and compelling one-of-a-kind stories. When the Center for Transforming Lives was still under the YWCA national umbrella, a local family loved the mission and offered a dollar-for-dollar match to permanently endow its Homeless Daycare Program.

The pitch to me was surely the Foundation could make an exception to the no endowment funding rule in order to secure permanent future support for homeless daycare. I said even one exception would lead to another and we were not going down that road. This was followed by, why can't you help us?

I never said we would not help, I just said we could not give to the endowment. I knew the organization counted on its annual Women Who Care Share fundraising luncheon for several hundred thousand dollars of operating support. I proposed putting every dollar raised at the luncheon that year toward the endowment match. Then, for that year only, ask the Foundation to replace the lost operating support.

This strategy helped them reach their endowment goal without disrupting current-year operating support. The following year they could return to business as usual without depending on the Foundation for operating support.

There is another cautionary endowment note tied to this example. When the Center for Transforming Lives was

breaking away from YWCA national, this restricted endowment fund proved to be a complicated challenge in determining who had legal ownership. ♀

ENDOWMENT FUNDING STRATEGY

Substitute funding offer— Child Study Center
(previously mentioned but worth repeating)

SINCE 1962 THE Child Study Center has provided diagnosis and treatment services to children who have, or are at risk for, developmental disabilities and related behavioral and emotional problems. It is one of the few centers in the nation offering multiple services to children and families under one roof regardless of ability to pay.

The organization was much beloved in Tarrant County and enjoyed broad support. Based on several donor comments, leadership recognized an opportunity to secure some targeted one-time endowment gifts. However, there was concern this would negatively impact annual operating support in the year of an endowment gift.

I told them not to worry. If the Child Study Center received an endowment gift equal to ten times or more of historical annual support, the Foundation would replace the lost operating support. This plan seemed like a good solution to me, but it did not work! None of these donors had any interest in the Carter Foundation "helping them" support the Child Study Center. Endowment gifts were received along with the regular support for operations.

Another cautionary example to be noted. The Child Study Center eventually merged into Cook Children's Medical Center. Services continue to be provided on an even larger scale, but the Child Study Center endowment and building all became part of Cook's Healthcare Foundation. ♀

ENDOWMENT FUNDING STRATEGY

First this, then endow—
First Tee—Fort Worth

THE FIRST TEE is a national program that began in 1997 to provide young people ages eight to eighteen from all backgrounds an introduction to golf as well as character education and life-enhancing skills and values. First Tee Life Skills emphasize nine core values—honesty, integrity, responsibility, respect, confidence, judgment, perseverance, courtesy, sportsmanship—and how these apply to everyday life.

First Tee—Fort Worth was a collaborative project with the City of Fort Worth Parks and Community Service Department along with youth-serving organizations including the Boys and Girls Clubs, United Community Centers, YMCA, Lena Pope Home and All Church Home.

The City provided land to build a practice area and Learning Center at one of the municipal golf courses. The site provided a home base for the program and a centralized location for the target audience.

First Tee—Fort Worth was successful in securing the necessary commitments to construct the Learning Center. However, they ran into a problem when notified that a $500,000 pledge would take several years before it would be funded.

First Tee approached the Foundation about a loan that could be repaid when the pledge was completed or to fund the gap needed to begin construction. Instead, we committed $250,000 to use as a challenge match to raise the remaining funds needed to build.

This approach was successful and enabled First Tee to move forward with construction. Plus, it provided a pathway to establish an endowment with the previous $500,000 commitment as those pledge payments were received. ♀

ENDOWMENT FUNDING STRATEGY

The easiest ways

NOTHING ABOUT ENDOWMENT funding is ever easy, but two of the simplest strategies involve integration into new building projects.

Most capital campaigns now include a maintenance reserve as part of the goal. Instead of carving it out as a separate line item, the endowment portion can simply be included in the project price. This results in a larger goal, but more donors will support an all-in building project rather than a smaller goal and a separate endowment component.

The second strategy is not quite as easy but very straightforward. If an organization is selling existing property in order to relocate, the sales proceeds are an ideal way to jump-start an endowment. I know most organizations count on these funds to offset a portion of new construction cost, but I believe donors will respond to helping with new construction knowing other funds have been set aside for the endowment. ♀

FINAL THOUGHTS ON CAPITAL CAMPAIGNS

The 99-cent rule still applies

THERE'S A GOOD reason why retailers have long relied on pricing items at a certain dollar amount plus 99 cents—because the price does not appear as high! The same approach applies to capital campaigns.

Psychologically, $9.9 million sounds less daunting than $10 million. Same goes for $975,000 instead of $1 million. Staying underneath that next significant round number gets things started on a more positive note. ♀

FINAL THOUGHTS ON CAPITAL CAMPAIGNS

Consistency

A CAPITAL CAMPAIGN will be the largest project organizations ever undertake. Thoughtful and comprehensive planning are essential. One absolutely critical element is everyone involved must be consistent in what is said regarding the cost of the project and the goal.

Whether coming from staff, Board members, volunteers, marketing pieces or publications, the campaign goal must be a consistent number. Prospective donors often compare notes, and the topic might come up in conversation. It is essential they have heard the same amount.

It's easy for things to get confusing if someone starts factoring in sales proceeds from something, in-kind contributions, pro bono services, New Market Tax Credits or whatever else might muddy the story. Remain clear, the campaign goal is X, we already have commitments of Y, and we still need to raise Z by a certain date.

With most projects, the contractor can determine when groundbreaking must happen for completion to occur by a certain date, such as the start of school. These target dates also need to be consistent so everyone is working with the same information.

Multiple stories or inconsistent amounts create confusion and raise the question of what is really needed. This one-number approach will need to be updated as commitments are received. News of additional gifts provides an opportunity to keep existing donors and prospects connected and informed about what's still needed to complete the project. ♀

OTHER EFFECTIVE IDEAS I HAVE SEEN BUT TAKE NO CREDIT FOR

Social media to stay connected

TRINITY HABITAT FOR Humanity's Executive Director is Gage Yager. For several years he had Gage's Tweet of the Week. Recognizing that not all of their donors were on Twitter (including me), the organization also emailed screenshots of the text to their mailing list.

To this day, I still recall one tweet saying simply, "Put a family of four in a new home today! They had been paying $879 in rent but now their mortgage is $500. On their way to financial success!" These weekly communications were not funding requests but a way to remind supporters of the agency's lasting impact.

There is no magic in weekly communications, but undeniable value exists in staying connected with donors throughout the year and not just with an annual report or when it's time to request additional support.

Social media is also a great way to communicate emergency needs. One year, Fort Worth experienced a major ice storm and the city just shut down. The Presbyterian Night Shelter broadcast an appeal for bottled water. It was not long before four-wheel drive vehicles with chains on their tires started showing up with cases and cases of water. This approach succeeded because the social media network had already been established. ♀

OTHER EFFECTIVE IDEAS I HAVE SEEN BUT TAKE NO CREDIT FOR

Provide something people value

THE DALLAS THEOLOGICAL Seminary (DTS) had a monthly publication called *Veritas*. Each edition featured articles on the Seminary, faculty members and some students, Bible study guides and quiet time devotionals. Anyone attending a Seminary event or providing an address went on the publication's mailing list. DTS found that after several months, people began sending contributions in the envelope included with the mailing. Consistently, the comments were, please keep me on the mailing list because this information is meaningful and valuable to me.

Any time an organization can provide knowledge and practical information that people find valuable, the likelihood of financial support increases. Help can take the form of educational stories, health information, cooking tips, parenting suggestions, relationship advice, etc. etc. etc.

DTS also was successful in converting many of its donors to Impact Partners, which involved making a three-year commitment. The Seminary continued to provide useful information and, along the way, would ask donors to renew their Impact Partner pledge. Personally, I became a supporter in 2003 and have no idea where I am in my current three-year pledge cycle, but it doesn't matter because I continue to love what they do. ♀

OTHER EFFECTIVE IDEAS I HAVE SEEN BUT TAKE NO CREDIT FOR

Know your audience

UNION GOSPEL MISSION held a dinner one night in honor of Ron Hall, one of their volunteers who had written the book *Same Kind of Different as Me*, the story of his relationship with Denver Moore, one of the homeless residents, while Ron and his wife volunteered at the shelter and later during her terminal illness.

The book was inspiring, and the evening was powerful and emotional. The evening was not intended to be a fundraising event, but there was a soft appeal at the end. Before I left, the Executive Director asked for my thoughts on how the night went.

I told him it was a fantastic evening but I did not think many of the attendees came prepared to write a $1,000+ check. I suggested that in the future, if an appeal was planned, a monthly pledge option might be something to consider.

As sometimes happens, he took my advice. The next mailer I received from Union Gospel Mission included twelve pre-addressed envelopes. It was several months before I saw the Executive Director again, and when I did I mentioned it was not necessary to mail envelopes. On the contrary, he said the response had been fantastic! Union Gospel had a new group of donors providing monthly support!

Meals on Wheels of Tarrant County told me that for several months after the 9-11 attack, monthly contributions from small donors completely disappeared. It was their assessment that this audience had a finite amount to contribute each month. After that horrific attack, this group shifted their available funds to organizations responding to that crisis. After about six months, those monthly contributors started returning to their favorite local causes.

I have one more thought on monthly givers. Large donors probably will not fund on a monthly basis. However, a much greater population lives on a budget and chooses to share resources out of available monthly income. These people writing monthly checks demonstrate that the organization is always in their heart. I'm not sure a recurring monthly debit carries the same emotional commitment. ♀

OTHER EFFECTIVE IDEAS I HAVE SEEN BUT TAKE NO CREDIT FOR

Unique events

CIRCLE OF FRIENDS provides volunteers, funding and assistance with programs that benefit children diagnosed through Cook Children's Medical Center with cancer and other illnesses. For several weeks each fall, this volunteer group comes together to transform plain pumpkins into holiday delights.

Talented artists paint, glaze and decorate pumpkins into remarkable works of art. These painted pumpkins are then sold or auctioned off to fund the Christmas drive for the patients at Cook Children's. In addition to the fundraising aspect, the pumpkins are so well done they become a topic of discussion when people see them, which presents yet another opportunity to raise awareness. Plus, since pumpkins have a limited shelf life, a new one must be purchased every year!

On more than one occasion, the Fort Worth Symphony Orchestra has used Painted Violins as a fundraiser for their Adventures in Music program, which brings symphonic music to thousands of children from all socioeconomic and cultural backgrounds. The Symphony reaches out to professional and celebrity artists to create original art pieces by painting unfinished violins. Each work of art is inspired by a specific composition or music in general.

Some of the painted violins have sold for significant sums and can be found hanging in homes and offices in shadow boxes or mounted directly on the wall. The artwork is beautiful, and each piece has a unique story behind it.

In December The WARM Place (What About Remembering Me) offers *A Phone Call From Santa* fundraiser. Each year over 100 volunteer Santas play the role of Jolly ol' Saint Nick. They make personalized phone calls to children across the country to keep the magic of Santa alive and spread holiday cheer.

Every call is truly personalized because the conversation is scripted based upon a completed form including the child's name as well as their siblings and pets, activities the past year, travel taken, grades in school, accomplishments and of course, what they want for Christmas. It always amazes the phone call recipients that Santa knows so much about them, and there is wonder and excitement when they hear, "Ho, Ho, Ho, Merry Christmas!"

OTHER EFFECTIVE IDEAS I HAVE SEEN BUT TAKE NO CREDIT FOR

Voting with dollars

STAGE WEST THEATRE developed a unique event, Acting with the Stars, to raise funds and broaden their audience reach. Success comes from the ability to identify high-profile people in the community who will agree to act in a two-person scene with a professional actor.

The volunteer commitment is not insignificant, with rehearsal time, costume fitting, makeup, stage blocking and other things I am not aware of. The night of the event features a nice dinner with a stage set in the middle followed by performances of these one-act scenes. The fundraising portion of the evening comes when the audience can vote for their favorite performance by contributing to the theatre. The actor raising the most money is recognized, but the real winner is Stage West.

Fort Worth Sister Cities hosts a similar event patterned after *Dancing with the Stars*. There is some disagreement over which event inspired the other!

The Ladies Auxiliary of Arlington has supported the Boys and Girls Clubs for over 64 years through the Cinderella Charity Ball. Each year twenty high school sophomore and junior girls in Arlington are selected as candidates based upon applications highlighting community and church activities, honors received and academic standing.

Each candidate then conducts her own seven-week campaign. Campaigns consist of individual mailings, telephone calls, fundraising events and speaking engagements. The appeals tell a little about the candidates and a lot about the Boys and Girls Clubs in Arlington. Each young lady creates her own mailing list of family, friends, community associates and business contacts, which helps the organization reach a wider audience each year.

Candidates then solicit contributions, which are counted as votes for them as Miss Cinderella. Funds raised go toward scholarships for children attending the Clubs as well as for the candidates. Through 2024, the Miss Cinderella Charity Ball has raised in excess of $16.2 million for the Boys and Girls Clubs in Arlington. ♀

OTHER EFFECTIVE IDEAS I HAVE SEEN BUT TAKE NO CREDIT FOR

Different ways to raise support

SUSAN G. KOMEN Greater Fort Worth had a fundraising event that would be hard to replicate. I do not believe the strategy was intentional, but the financial success exceeded all expectations.

The concept was a two-day, online fundraiser involving the husbands of Komen Board members. To encourage participation, several unique, and possibly coveted, items would be won by those individuals raising the most money.

What no one anticipated was several of the men wanting the *second-place* prize — a highly desirable hunting trip. As the contributions being raised were reported in real time online, several guys started contributing to each other in an effort to put someone else in first place and move them into second.

Interesting idea to have the most wanted prize to not be for first place!

I was peripherally involved in this next idea but it did not involve the Foundation. During COVID, all benefit dinners came to a halt. A friend of mine had been selected to receive the Boy Scouts Distinguished Citizen Award. I told him the Scouts made a good choice but he should ask to be deferred for a year in order to have a successful event.

Since the annual operating budget was counting on this event, I suggested he float the idea of having the Boy Scouts write an appeal letter explaining what they were doing during the pandemic and why continued support was warranted.

Further, have the past five recipients of the Distinguished Citizen Award sign the letter.

That letter alone brought in 95% of the budgeted gross revenue, and since there were no dinner expenses, the net income made it even more successful. The next year my friend was recognized and the evening proceeds set a fundraising record! ♀

OTHER EFFECTIVE IDEAS I HAVE SEEN BUT TAKE NO CREDIT FOR

Seeing firsthand— Cook Children's Medical Center

UNLESS THERE WAS a birth, wedding or funeral, I doubt anyone can say without looking back at a daytimer what they were doing January 21, 2004. Twenty-plus years later, I don't need any notes to remember exactly what I was doing from 6 a.m. to 9 p.m. that day.

Cook Children's Medical Center invited me to be part of a beta-test group for a new program called Experience the Mission. The concept was to have community leaders and donors spend an entire day seeing the inside operation of the hospital.

This program was not a group exercise. Each person had four randomly assigned rotations accompanied by a hospital employee to chronicle the day's events. Since this was an experiment, I understood the logic of having an employee shadow us in case of a fainting spell or being overwhelmed by what we saw. It's amusing to think back on that day when pictures had to be taken with a disposable camera and then have the film developed.

Experience the Mission started the evening before with an orientation on what the next day would entail. We received our own scrubs with Experience the Mission on them so we would not be confused with people who knew what they were doing.

My rotations included an eye surgery where the eyeball was distended from the socket to correct a lazy eye; hand surgery resulting from a skateboard accident; pre-op and post-op care and how parents were included in the lead-up to surgery and then recovery; kidney dialysis; and being present for the heartbreaking message that a childhood brain tumor had returned to a young lady. In the evening there was a debriefing and closing dinner with the hospital employees we had spent the day with experiencing the mission.

Other members in the program that day spent time in the Emergency Department, neonatal unit and a variety of operating rooms. What I observed and learned will be with me forever. My respect and appreciation for what physicians, nurses, child life specialists and administrators at Cook Children's do every day for these children and their families could not be any greater.

Experience the Mission has now expanded into virtually every aspect of the hospital. I'm confident that everyone who has experienced the mission is now both an advocate for and donor to Cook Children's. ♀

OTHER EFFECTIVE IDEAS I HAVE SEEN BUT TAKE NO CREDIT FOR

Everybody wins!

ACQUIRING PROPERTY FOR continued growth is always a challenge. One of the most compassionate and effective strategies I have seen involved approaching property owners and offering them the opportunity to find another home in the area. Their new home could be larger, in a better location, and probably on a quieter street. With some generous pricing parameters, the new home would be purchased by the nonprofit and then traded to the homeowner(s) for their existing property.

No one was ever forced out but it was a compelling opportunity for homeowners to upgrade at no cost, and the needed property could be secured. ♀

OTHER EFFECTIVE IDEAS I HAVE SEEN BUT TAKE NO CREDIT FOR

Raise money the old-fashioned way—just bill them!

ALTHOUGH NOT A charitable deduction, many country clubs and city clubs have scholarship funds for their employees or employees' children. Additional benefits such as this are an effective away of attracting and retaining staff.

For years clubs reached out to select members to help with special situations. Now most private clubs have a voluntary, but strongly encouraged Christmas contribution. I now see midsummer line items added to monthly statements for things like scholarship funding.

If this approach seems too aggressive, another option is having an additional line on the membership or dues statement with the option to voluntarily support specific initiatives. ♀

CONCLUSION

Six R's of Effective Fundraising

NOW THAT YOU'VE been introduced to 100-plus ways to be inspired and all types of new ideas and strategies, new funding sources are needed. Caveat No. 1 is the Amon G. Carter Foundation cannot be the answer for everyone!

However, I have developed what I consider the Six R's of Effective Fundraising for groups planning to approach foundations and trusts. I'm not promising these steps will be easy, but I do believe they work.

1) **Research**

    Before asking, spend time learning about a funder's areas of interest, average size grant, request requirements, deadlines and Board members.

2) **Relationships**

    It's not necessary to be best friends, but you need to find a way to be introduced and meet face to face (or at least speak with someone) before submitting a proposal. I know many funders do not offer a pathway to arrange a meeting, but your chances greatly increase when there has been some type of interaction.

3) **Real Estate**

    Site visits are the most effective way to connect with funders. When someone can see the program in action and the faces of the people being helped, funding prospects go way up.

4) **Rationale**

There needs to be a specific reason to compel funding a request besides the generalization that the organization is doing good work and needs financial assistance. Again, the relationship aspect will help guide the request toward an area of interest.

5) **Realistic**

Requests should be for an amount the funder can approve. It is not a successful strategy to seek a larger amount expecting to receive something less. To repeat, having a relationship will help avoid a misstep of asking for the wrong amount.

6) **Report Back**

This is the one area often overlooked. Whether or not a grant is approved, organizations should remain in contact and provide updates on how things are going. In the case of capital campaigns, those who have committed will want to know the current status in case someone asks (funders do talk to other funders). If a request was declined, it might not have been the right time due to other funding commitments. By keeping everyone apprised of the progress, additional funding might come in the future.

FINAL INSPIRATION

Handwritten thank you notes are becoming a thing of the past. However, they always stand out, and their personalized nature will draw attention to your organization. To emphasize how effective they are with me, I keep them.

If handwritten notes are not feasible, at a minimum do include a short, personalized note on the bottom of correspondence with your donors. It will be noticed. ♀

Part Two

Grantmaking Ideas

GRANTMAKING THOUGHTS TO CONSIDER

Introduction

As MENTIONED IN the Introduction, I have had the privilege of working for the Amon G. Carter Foundation for 45 years. Since 1997 my responsibilities have included meeting with all organizations seeking funding. During my tenure the Foundation's annual grant budget has grown from $5 million in 1981 to almost $40 million in 2025.

In addition to the Amon G. Carter Foundation, the Amon G. Carter Star-Telegram Employees Fund was established in 1949 to respond to a devastating flood in Fort Worth when many of Mr. Carter's employees lost their homes. Even though Carter Publications was sold in 1974, the Employees Fund continues to provide benefits to those employed at the time of sale. Along with its primary mission of assisting retirees with medical hardships, the endowment has grown to a size allowing for a community grants program as well. I also oversee this $2 million-plus community grant budget.

No one should be giving away other people's money without demonstrating personal philanthropy. My career has enabled my wife and me to share in the joy and satisfaction associated with individual giving.

I mention these aspects of grantmaking experience only to establish some credibility for why my ideas might be worth considering. Most people believe I have one of the greatest jobs in the world. I do not disagree, but my day-to-day activities are not what people think. I meet with many organizations addressing heartbreaking issues that no amount of money can fix. Finding some way to offer advice and support to them all is the most challenging thing I do.

My pastor asked, "What gets you up in the morning?" I told him it did not have as much do with money as people would think. I went on to say that I thought people came to see me with the expectation I would have ideas for them and ask questions they had not considered even though that is what they do every day. What gets me up in the morning is meeting or exceeding those expectations. The day the only question I ask is, "How much money do you need?" is the day my grantmaking is over.

On the following pages I share some of my experiences and lessons learned. I hope some of them become Your Next Inspiration for Grantmaking Ideas. ♀

VENN DIAGRAMS SHOULD BE APPLIED TO PHILANTHROPY

EFFECTIVE PHILANTHROPY INVOLVES empathy, understanding, passion, and a brain-based evaluation of the situation. The most impactful grantmaking comes from where the heart and mind intersect. It should never be just one or the other. ♀

SOME ADAGES DO
REMAIN TRUE

ONE ADAGE OFTEN repeated is, "If you have seen one, you have seen them all." When it comes to foundations and grantmaking, "If you have seen one, you have seen one!" The one thing foundations have in common is they do things their way and not necessarily like anyone else. Even given this limitation, I believe the information here can inspire every grantmaker, as something to consider doing—or to decide never to do.

Another adage is, if you ask for funding, you will probably get advice. However, if you start by asking for advice, you might get funding.

Most requests for appointments with the Carter Foundation begin with the premise of looking for advice. I think the thought process is surely a funder will want to support their own advice so that it will be successful.

The most terrifying words I hear are, "*We took your advice.*" My mind immediately goes to what selective hearing was involved, or what I could have said that was interpreted as the way to proceed.

Like every example in this book, I try to convey that my ideas may sound good during the meeting, but each group must evaluate what advice will work best in their situation. ♀

WHAT DO I EXPECT FROM MYSELF AS A GRANTMAKER?

EVERYONE I MEET with is passionate about the cause being discussed. For many it is their career and livelihood. For others, a significant investment of personal time, talent and resources has already been made.

In addition to funding, I believe people sincerely want advice. They want to succeed in their endeavors and learn what else they should do and who else they should contact. They seek counsel on ways to improve their presentation in order to be better received by other potential funders.

I meet with CEOs more often than with Development Directors. It is appropriate for some conversations to begin with just one person from the organization, but the most productive meetings usually involve more than one. Having representation from some combination of leadership from administration, development, programming and the Board provides an opportunity for discussion that includes multiple perspectives.

I try to ask questions during the meeting about aspects of the program that need clarification. After hearing countless presentations, if I have a question, I suspect other potential funders will want that information as well. I ask questions to better understand the organization but also to help prepare them to incorporate that information into future presentations.

I also recommend not trying to predetermine where a funder's interest will be. It is better to offer a menu of ideas and opportunities. There is a much higher likelihood one area will resonate for a reason no one could have anticipated. The menu approach also opens the door for discussions about what can be accomplished at different funding levels.

I always ask about who they partner with in providing service to the community. I am amazed how frequently proposals lack that information. While I'm looking for uniqueness and unduplicated efforts, I am always interested in who they get referrals from and who they work with to provide a continuum of care. I also want to know what others think of the program and if the organization has a reputation for doing what they say they will do. ♀

REPUTATION AND KNOWING WHAT OTHERS THINK ABOUT AN ORGANIZATION

ONE EXAMPLE I frequently share involves the Neuhaus Education Center. Neuhaus is based in Houston, and one of their main programs involves providing dyslexia training for teachers to help them recognize and assist students with this learning difference.

I first received a cold call from Neuhaus seeking funding to bring more dyslexia training to teachers in North Texas. I told them that although I considered this a worthwhile goal, what I thought really didn't matter. I did not fund projects just because I felt it was important. It needed to be embraced by those who would receive the training. In other words, I would need to meet with Neuhaus *and* the school district desiring the services. Neuhaus responded that would not be a problem since they already had existing working relationships.

Before the Neuhaus follow-up appointment, I was in a meeting with the Key School, which serves students with a variety of learning differences. During that discussion I asked Key School representatives if they were familiar with the Neuhaus Education Center. Their response was an enthusiastic, "They are the best!" Key relied on Neuhaus training every year and attributed some of their success with students to the instruction Neuhaus provided.

Nothing Neuhaus could have said carried as much weight as this partner testimonial. When I did meet with Neuhaus, I listened with a much more receptive attitude based on Key School's glowing recommendation. ♀

REFERENCES ARE IMPORTANT

WHENEVER I MEET with an organization I always encourage them to include a list of other service providers they partner with. This addendum in their information packet also should include individual names and contact information.

As noted in the previous example, nothing carries more weight than having another organization affirm how important the requesting group is to its success in serving the community. These references can confirm how others view the organization, the length of time they have worked together, and whether the organization is integral to the continuum of care in the community.

Since most funders support numerous organizations, it is likely some of the names on the partner reference list will be known to them. A more complete understanding of this network of service providers may encourage additional support in an area where a funder has already demonstrated interest.

I never cease to be amazed how many direct and indirect referrals and relationships exist that organizations never think about including in proposals. ♀

COORDINATE EFFORTS TO MAXIMIZE IMPACT

THE LEARNING CENTER of North Texas (now LinkED) offered summer training for teachers called Schools Attuned. This effective program helped teachers recognize different learning styles and adapt their teaching techniques to help individual students succeed.

The program worked great for individual teachers, but unless a coordinated effort was made for continuity between grade levels, student achievement gains might be lost the following year unless the next teacher had also received the training.

Initially, the Foundation paid half of the training cost, with the balance coming from the school district or teacher receiving the training. It did not take long to realize the program worked only if individual schools had a multi-year plan to train the first-grade teachers, then the second grade, etc.

The schools with the best articulated plans were the ones we supported. ♀

FREE THINGS ARE OFTEN NOT VALUED

PEOPLE NEED MANY things, but when those things are received solely out of generosity, sometimes they're not valued. Individuals may have limited resources, but there are other ways for them to have buy-in to a program. As an example, the Foundation was asked to provide funding for the PSAT examination fee so every tenth-grader in a school district could take the test.

I recognized the idea had merit for the students as well as the district because everyone would get a better idea of areas where students were excelling as well as deficient. I also knew that not every student could afford the fee. Instead of simply covering the cost, I suggested the students could earn the fee by attending several preparation classes. This approach proved to provide a better outcome rather than just having students show up and take a free test. ♀

COMPETE FOR FUNDING TO FEEL AWARDED, NOT ENTITLED

NONPROFITS PROVIDE MANY programs to schools. As long as a program is free, more often than not school principals will gladly accept. In my experience, what is free is often not valued.

Since resources will always be limited, I look for programs where a provider wants to go into several pilot schools. Instead of the school district choosing the locations, I have seen much greater success when schools compete to be chosen. Each principal must propose what his or her school will do to maximize success if it is selected. This front-end competition and buy-in works so well because all parties are invested and want to see positive outcomes. ♀

PARTICIPATION ENCOURAGES SUCCESS

THE RIVER LEGACY Foundation in Arlington provides extraordinary outdoor learning experiences. During a meeting with them, our discussion centered on their plans to develop a curriculum to engage more teenagers.

I suggested River Legacy reach out to teachers at their partner schools and ask each to nominate several students to serve on a committee to develop input for the curriculum. What better people to ask than the audience you're trying to reach?

This approach had multiple positive implications. First, teachers felt valued by being asked for their involvement. Second, they were now invested by proactively choosing which students would represent them and their school in the project. And finally, the students felt honored to have been selected to participate in a citywide project. Not to mention, the experience provided great college essay material!

The personal pride that comes from feeling part of something important leads to much higher levels of involvement and engagement. ♀

EVERY GRANT SETS
AN EXAMPLE

A BASIC FUNDRAISING strategy involves researching funders and their areas of interest. Once a category of past giving is identified, funders will probably receive more requests for that area. I point out that when organizations donate an item to one school, they should expect solicitations from other schools for a similar gift. Likewise, the funding amount will guide others to seek same-sized grants.

This information is meant to be cautionary, not discouraging. Every gift becomes part of a giving database that will be researched in the future. Organizations continue to invite me to visit historic properties because they have discovered we funded such requests sometime in the past. ♀

RIGHTSIZING A GRANT FOR PERCEPTION

RECOVERY RESOURCE COUNCIL offers a number of programs to address substance abuse, addiction and mental health for the general population with special emphasis on veterans. The Carter Foundation has supported the organization over the years with pilot programs, expansion of existing services and facility improvements.

One year we made a grant to address security needs and replace windows fronting a highway for sound and efficiency. Before the windows were ordered, the organization learned that the roadway would be widened and its building taken through eminent domain.

Recovery Resource notified me of the change in plans and asked if our grant could be redirected toward a planned capital campaign in Dallas to purchase and renovate a building. My response was no for the capital campaign but I then asked how much expense had been incurred for architectural and engineering planning. I went on to explain that a $75,000 grant from the Carter Foundation that paid for half of the planning cost sent an entirely different message than a gift of that amount toward a multimillion-dollar building capital campaign.

Being intentional about the optics of where our funding was directed helped demonstrate the importance of the project to us. Funding 50% of the planning portion versus 3% of the capital campaign helped Recovery Resource communicate to Dallas funders how we viewed the initiative. ♀

UNDERSTANDING THE CHALLENGES TO HELPING OTHERS

Donna Floyd founded a nonprofit called Justin's Place. The genesis came from her idea to take a Vacation Bible School type program into a low-income community. Once there, she discovered virtually all of the children were from single-mother homes and faced numerous challenges trying to change their life trajectory.

Donna tells the story that when she was a little girl, she knew her parents loved her because they told her. Every night they read to her, prayed with her, and she went to sleep knowing she was safe and loved. Then, when she had children of her own, she replicated the model she knew by telling her children they were loved. Every night she read to them, prayed with them, and *they* went to sleep knowing they were safe and loved.

The women Donna encountered through Justin's Place may have wanted to be good mothers but did not know how because they had no positive examples to emulate. The women who wanted something different were like sponges soaking up information about ways to think and live.

Donna's story reminds me that helping others out of poverty is challenging because even those individuals who want something better may not have a framework of understanding the importance of relationships, nurturing, education, commitment, goal setting, work ethic, health, respect for others and respect for authority. ♀

TESTING THE WATER

SUCCESSFUL NONPROFITS OFTEN run out of space and want to consider buying or constructing a new or larger building. Often this relocation will involve moving operations to a different area.

When Catholic Charities Fort Worth was planning their move, I suggested renting space in the area where they intended to build. This way they could confirm if clients would be comfortable coming to a different location. In this case it turned out client visits increased which confirmed their relocation plans and helped build the case for their capital campaign. The planned site was actually a better place to provide services and Catholic Charities knew going in that the location would be accepted, utilized and attract even more people in need. The pilot site confirmed they were moving in the right direction, and strengthened their fundraising story.

Any time a funder can help a nonprofit develop a capital campaign plan like this that increases the probability of success, they should encourage (and possibly even participate in) a pilot location. ♀

FEASIBILITY STUDIES SERVE NUMEROUS PURPOSES

MANY ORGANIZATIONS MAY only conduct one capital campaign—ever. Even established nonprofits should consider having an outside consultant conduct a feasibility study. In my experience, few people will be completely candid with a leader or Board member of an organization. Human nature does not lend itself to raising issues and squashing dreams of the people working with a nonprofit organization every day.

An outside consultant is more likely to hear honest feedback regarding questions and concerns about a proposed expansion. It is crucial to have a skilled individual do the feasibility study who can help prepare the case study, answer anticipated questions and have access to key decision makers who will help determine the success of the endeavor.

A good feasibility consultant is not there to be a cheerleader but to give honest feedback about questions asked and a realistic assessment of what can be accomplished. ♀

PROVIDING A SAFETY NET CAN ENCOURAGE MORE CREATIVE THINKING

As ALREADY MENTIONED, I prefer to help nonprofits find new ways to support themselves. In this example the concept sounds dated and hard to imagine in today's environment, but at the time it was a creative option.

Fundraising dinners have always been held to honor outstanding individuals in a community. The YWCA of Fort Worth and Tarrant County came up with a unique spin on that idea by asking downtown companies to identify one female employee who had made an exceptional contribution during the past year. The YWCA hoped local businesses would nominate someone, then buy a table for a luncheon where the nominees would be recognized and awards given.

I was asked what I thought about the idea and if they could count on the Foundation to be a safety net in case the event fell flat. In this instance, we were not asked to be a sponsor but to evaluate projected budget scenarios and participation levels along with the fixed costs incurred regardless of response.

The inaugural event proved to be very popular and grew to be a significant fundraiser for the YWCA. Eventually, the event morphed into a different format for just female employees called Women Who Care Share.

We never had to provide any funding, but knowing they could not lose money encouraged the YWCA to move forward and try something different. ♀

SAFETY NET 2.0 WITH AN UNEXPECTED LESSON LEARNED

ONE OF THE unique things on my résumé is being a twenty-plus-year Advisor to the Junior League of Fort Worth. Like most organizations, they were looking for a fresh fundraising idea. They researched Junior League events around the country and focused on creating their own version of successful ideas from other cities.

They settled on an October event, Christmas in Cowtown, which would give its members (and the community) an early start on Christmas shopping by having vendors set up booths and sell a wide variety of items.

During the planning process they developed sponsorship opportunities, preview events, early entry shopping times and ticket sales for premium events to be held Thursday through Sunday. Again, the Foundation was approached to be a safety net but, in this case, it made more sense to have our name listed as a sponsor.

The event was enthusiastically received and has since become a Fort Worth mainstay. I include this example because the only disappointment the Junior League committee had after the first year's event was not securing a title sponsor. I told the organizers that this might seem strange but I was glad no one stepped up with $25,000 that first year. Instead, I was pleased the Junior League had so many $1,000, $2,500 and $5,000 sponsors, which signaled broad support for the cause.

If there had been a title sponsor that first year, the pressure on the following year's committee to secure a gift at least that size would have been the sole determining factor if the event was a success. Having a broad base of lower level support ensured enthusiasm, participation and signaled the event was financially healthy.

A DIFFERENT KIND OF
SAFETY NET

Bridge Funding

As a REMINDER, the purpose of these examples is to encourage a variety of ways to consider helping organizations you want to assist. Obviously, all organizations require operating support to deliver their programs, and there's nothing wrong with providing unrestricted funds for operations. My only caution is that unless you can maintain that support every year, any disruption may harm the enterprise.

There are numerous scenarios where organizations have absolutely no control over losing program funding. I have seen program funding from the State of Texas lost due to an unintentional change in the wording of a statute. And, of course, federal guidelines are constantly changing. Or a funder's financial situation changes and they are unable to fulfill a funding commitment.

I will consider bridge funding to prevent the disruption of a critical program if the shortfall is temporary, or a reasonable plan exists to replace the support. Bridge funding as a safety net can be invaluable as long as the organization can demonstrate a pathway out of reliance on the Carter Foundation for ongoing operations. ♀

ONE MORE SAFETY NET STRATEGY

Loan Repayment

SOME FUNDERS HAVE a philosophy of not providing grants for debt service. Encouraging nonprofits to be debt free is always preferable. However, any organization that has debt also has money from some source going toward debt service.

Here are two examples where our participation specifically targeted debt issues.

HOPE Farm, an outstanding program serving fatherless boys, has a multipurpose building that houses education classrooms and a gymnasium. The roof was severely damaged in a horrific hail storm. Fortunately, the organization had replacement value insurance, but it came with a very large deductible.

HOPE Farm leadership was not comfortable dipping that far into reserves for this unexpected summertime expenditure. The Foundation was approached to help fund the repair since many other donors were already committed to a separate capital campaign on another campus.

I told them we wanted to help but our next grant meeting was not until November and our guidelines prohibited making a gift that large between meetings. Since the organization planned to borrow the money, I said I'd be happy to talk to their loan officer about our intentions and timeline. This strategy to provide funding for loan repayment allowed the repairs to move forward during downtime in the summer and not disrupt the program's impact during the school year.

Separately, we also got involved with debt retirement during the pandemic. As some nonprofits struggled to stay afloat, we provided grants to cover monthly mortgage payments so other donations could go to program services. In one situation we retired the remaining debt so that the amounts previously used for monthly mortgage payments could permanently be redirected toward operations. ♀

SUPPORTING FUNDRAISING EVENTS

FUNDERS ARE NOT allowed to receive any personal benefit from grants made by a foundation. Even though we cannot attend, the Carter Foundation provides support for several events each year. Event underwriting usually occurs in years where we are not providing any other grant support. Our rationale is there is value for the organization in having our name listed as a sponsor and demonstrating support for their efforts.

Some donors may not attend but specify their table can be used by the nonprofit's employees or for other guests of the charity. One year we provided support for a performing arts event and designated our gift for use by Board members of the charity to invite guests they thought might want to learn more about the organization. Board members are usually the first ask for many types of financial support, but for once they could just host others and promote the charity they were passionate about helping. ♀

SMALL GRANTS CAN MAKE A WORLD OF DIFFERENCE

LARGE GIFTS GET most of the publicity (and adulation), but smaller grants can have a different kind of impact and generate the most heartfelt appreciation.

One longtime Carter Foundation Board member, Dr. Robert W. "Bobby" Brown, had an amazing career and lifetime of accomplishments. He is honored in three college baseball Halls of Fame (Stanford, UCLA and Tulane) and attended medical school while playing for the New York Yankees!

Each year Bobby joined the Yankees after spring training when his academic semester ended and then had to catch up during fall classes after the baseball season ended (usually with the Yankees winning the World Series). He still holds several major league records but his baseball playing days were cut short when he began his residency in cardiology.

After a distinguished career as a cardiologist, he became President of the American League. While in that role representing major league baseball, he received many requests from small towns to support their Little League programs. When he joined the Foundation Board, we began setting aside designated funds to continue helping Boys and Girls Clubs, YMCAs and other nonprofit youth sports organizations.

Each year the Foundation would make fifteen to twenty grants, from $1,000 to $5,000, out of a $75,000 restricted fund to pay for bats, balls, gloves, uniforms and enrollment fees for programs in low-income communities. The number of people benefited is incalculable, but I have no doubt the children, their families and volunteer coaches stretched those funds farther than I ever could imagine.

And to reinforce how a small amount can deliver a major impact, over thirty-eight years we helped 160 programs, some numerous times, with grants totaling $2,589,030! ♀

PILOT PROGRAMS

SOME FUNDERS ARE more risk averse and prefer to not take a chance that their money might be wasted if something goes wrong. That approach is certainly fine, but I hope they will be more receptive once they see positive outcomes. The Carter Foundation will consider something new or different, providing there is a continuation plan that does not depend solely on us.

One example is marketing. Organizations always want ways to broaden awareness and their support base. If they have a realistic idea and can justify how they arrived at their new approach (or approaches), I probably will be interested in finding out if it works. I always emphasize that I do not expect things to go exactly as planned. Pilot programs provide an opportunity for modifications before moving forward. Beta testing with a smaller, target group also should be considered as part of a pilot.

Many times, nonprofits attempting to help people out of poverty, homelessness or some financial situation develop multi-week programs to help modify behavior. When the approach is new or unproven, I encourage them to emphasize this is a pilot program—lessons will be learned and course corrections needed to operate efficiently in the future. One of the most compelling storylines for funders is, "This is what we learned during the pilot, and this is what we're going to do differently because of our experience."

In building relationships with grant recipients, it is imperative they feel free to be honest about what happened instead of fearing repercussions from something that did not go exactly as planned. It's even better when course corrections begin as early as possible instead of waiting until the initial grant period ends.

Some grant agreements may stipulate that a program will serve a certain number of clients during a specified time. If early pilot results indicate the goal was too ambitious, personally I want to know as soon as possible instead of continuing down the road knowing the results will not be there. ♀

WHAT IS ON THE MENU?

ONE OF THE biggest challenges fundraisers face is trying to determine what to request and how much they can get. Again, every situation is different, but I encourage organizations to have a list of their programs and a menu of opportunities. Some requests will be modest while others will be very much the opposite.

By presenting an array of options, funders can focus on areas that fit their giving interests. I encourage groups I meet with to present a menu because no one can know what else we are considering at any given time. My default example has been that we have helped organizations improve their website design and functionality.

On most of our grant meeting agendas, there will be one (and only one) recommendation for marketing assistance that may include website enhancements. An organization requesting only website support has no idea who their competition is for that one spot. If I'm presented with a menu of opportunities, it is more likely I can find another area that is a fit for us and a way to help. Plus, receiving funding for another menu item might free up internal dollars to meet that website need if no one else provides that support.

One strategic grantmaking concept to consider is not selecting the "easy" request. I recognize some donors are more comfortable responding to certain types of straightforward needs. I prefer not to take those off the menu, knowing someone else might only fund that specific type of item. ♀

COMMUNICATION AMONG FUNDERS IS A GOOD THING

ON A LIGHTER (but still very serious) note, funders should never hesitate to discuss a project with their colleagues. I'm not promoting collusion but rather coordination as to timing and interest. In sharing this example, let me be clear that I do not condone anyone else trying this, and I hope never to experience anything like it again!

A nonprofit we had occasionally supported over the years approached me with a $6 million capital campaign. I said that was a very ambitious goal and asked what was their strategy to raise that much money? Their response was they intended to ask an "Un-named Foundation" for half. My reaction was, "Wow!" I know those guys and that would be the largest gift they had ever made. Who else were they planning to approach?

Instead of answering, the nonprofit pivoted the conversation to, "If we can raise $5.5 million, can we count on you for the last $500,000?" I said absolutely, come back when you have secured the other commitments.

Several months went by and I received a letter requesting $500,000 since commitments had been secured for the balance of funding. I happened to run into another funder I did not know well but knew his foundation had supported the organization in the past. I asked if he was helping with this $6 million campaign, and he said yes, he had agreed to contribute the last $500,000 if the nonprofit could raise the other $5.5 million! This organization had identified twelve historical funders with the capacity to make a gift of this size and gotten each to agree to be the last $500,000.

My lesson learned was to pick up the phone and talk to my colleagues and not rely solely on what the organization said was happening. In this case, all of the funders fulfilled their promise and the building was completed, but not surprisingly, the nonprofit has not been back. ♀

FUNDERS <u>DO NOT</u> ALWAYS KNOW BEST

FUNDERS FOR THE most part have found success doing something that lets them share their resources with others. One of the most difficult lessons to learn is just because a person with the money wants to do something to make a difference, there's no assurance that plan will work. The people responsible for executing the vision must share in the passion and not just be going through the motions because that's where the funding was supposed to be spent.

I have seen the most success when the group proposing to do the work brings the idea forward with a strategy to effectively reach the intended audience. Programs targeted to a population the funder does not deeply understand rarely hit the mark.

As a grantmaker, look to work with people and groups who have experience in that area. Give them freedom to challenge and modify ideas you may have on how to have the greatest impact. What makes good sense to you might completely miss the mark in a different socioeconomic or cultural situation. ♀

GRANTMAKERS NEED TO KEEP CURRENT

A SNAPSHOT OF what you remember from the past about an organization may no longer be accurate. Before making another gift, it is important to find out about things that might have affected the organization since your last involvement.

Have there been any changes in operations due to demand, staff turnover or revenue? What new opportunities have been identified? Any new partnerships? Understanding the current situation—not the one you think you know from before—helps determine a rationale for effective grantmaking.

To repeat, when you have a relationship with an organization and understand its operations and needs, it is much easier to identify how and where to assist with things that have a start and an end, like incentive grants, facility maintenance, marketing efforts or technology improvements. ♀

SOLVE A PROBLEM BY DIVIDING IT UP

A SMALL PERFORMING arts group approached me in a panic because a $10,000 grant they were anticipating fell through. Their initial reaction was to ask me to replace this lost funding. That approach would solve the immediate need but not address the issue for next year.

I suggested they not look for a single donor but instead encourage each Board member to identify $100, $250 and $500 contributors who could continue to support the organization and hopefully become ticket buyers. Their Board members bought into this divide and conquer strategy, especially when I offered to match all new donations up to the $10,000. This approach solved an immediate problem, helped establish a little reserve, and gave the organization a fundraising head start for the following year. ♀

TWO THINGS I THINK ABOUT ALL THE TIME

EVERYONE I MEET with is passionate about the cause he or she has come to discuss. (Almost) without exception, everything the Foundation hears about is worthwhile and our funding would make a difference.

For many it is a personal calling. Others have invested serious personal time and resources into the organization. Everyone seeking funding thinks grant approval offers a seal of approval that will validate them with other potential donors. Some have even said, "Can you give us something so we can at least use your name?"

All funding should be thoughtful and done with confidence that the project merits having your name being associated with it. On the other hand, declinations can be very damaging and send a message that something is wrong with the project or organization.

In our case, we communicate that if something does not rise to the priority to be included on one of the next two agendas, we are not able to help. I try to avoid formal declination letters in order to not further complicate an organization's fundraising efforts by having to say the Carter Foundation turned us down. ♀

TWO MORE THINGS I THINK ABOUT ON THE OTHER END OF THE SPECTRUM

WHILE SOME GRANT requests might not be a good fit for the Carter Foundation, others are exactly what we want to support. Sometimes, because of the nature of the program, the need for ongoing support will never go away. I do not have a solution for this situation other than to be aware of the level of funding and recognize what you're getting into regarding future needs and expectations.

Another complicating factor is scalability. If a program has outstanding results and legitimate justification for expansion, determining the right amount of support for the appropriate amount of time can be challenging. Hopefully, proven concepts will attract other donors, but the need for philanthropic support will never end. ♀

DEPTH OF ORGANIZATION TALENT SHOULD BE A FACTOR

No MATTER HOW good the idea or how great the reputation, organizations are run by people. Regardless of resources, we must depend on the character and capability of the people in charge to execute the strategy and manage the organization.

Executive Directors and Chief Executive Officers of non-profits have a difficult job. They are expected to be experts in their field as well as in budgeting, finance, fundraising, technology, risk management, human resources, facilities management, *and* be able to manage Type A Board members.

It's unrealistic to expect anyone to be great at everything, so it is important to know what type of talent they have around them both within the organization and on the Board.

One warning sign is frequent turnover at the top. Do not ignore it. ♀

FOUR REASONS FOR GIVING

STUDIES HAVE CONCLUDED that giving often falls into three categories:

1) Giving out of guilt or obligation is the most basic.

2) Recognition for the gift or to help an important cause is a little better reason.

3) Altruistic giving, because it is the right thing to do whether anyone knows about it or not, is the highest level.

People give for another reason that is sometimes overlooked. Having the right person present the request can make all the difference in the world! ♀

GEOGRAPHY IS OFTEN OVERLOOKED

I ENCOURAGE ORGANIZATIONS to keep a map handy of the city or county that shows where their planned location or service area will be. This visual helps them (and me) identify other resources (or lack thereof) in the area. When I ask smaller nonprofits for this information, they often are surprised to learn of other providers already in the area.

On a smaller scale, even seeing the site plans for a building or expansion can help me understand the need for requested funding. I typically ask for bullet points to be added on these documents to highlight additional services that will be provided in a new or expanded location. ♀

DILEMMAS AND DECISIONS

I HEARD A presentation at a Philanthropy Southwest meeting given by the Institute for Global Ethics based in Camden, Maine. I think these points are worth considering in grant-making decisions.

Right-versus-Right Dilemma Paradigms

- Truth versus Loyalty
- Short term versus Long term
- Justice versus Mercy
- Self versus Community

Decision Rules

- Ends Based: The greatest good for the greatest number
- Rules Based: A suitable rule for everyone to follow in similar situations
- Care Based: The Golden Rule

Making grant decisions among competing requests usually requires applying these filters. ♀

UNDERSTANDING AN AUDIENCE YOU MIGHT NOT BE FAMILIAR WITH

TARRANT COUNTY COLLEGE invited me to be on a scholarship review panel one year. I felt qualified and looked forward to the opportunity since I had years of experience on the scholarship committee for children of newspaper employees through the Amon G. Carter Star-Telegram Employees Fund.

TCC had many scholarship applicants representing, as one might expect, a range of high school grades and standardized test scores along with an interesting variety of experiences shared in the submissions.

One young woman's application really stood out from the others. However, it included a brief reference that she was dealing with a difficult first-trimester pregnancy. Since her submission was dated in May, according to my calculation the baby would be due in early October so I did not consider her a candidate for the fall semester.

During the scholarship discussion meeting, to my surprise I was the only one who did not rank her a top prospect. I pointed out that she would miss too much school with the birth of her child in the middle of the semester. I was politely corrected that in her circumstance, she would miss two days of class at the most. Good reminder for me, and another lesson learned. ♀

UNDERSTANDING A
TARGET AUDIENCE

RUBY K. PAYNE wrote an excellent book, *A Framework for Understanding Poverty*. Hearing her speak, and reading her book, gave me an entirely new perspective on how people in poverty face challenges virtually unknown to those in the middle or upper class. She emphasizes how being poor produces a survival mentality that turns attention away from opportunities most people take for granted.

Ms. Payne inspired me to incorporate into my grant-making filter how poverty impacts learning, decision making, incentives and work habits. Any proposal seeking to address a low-income population or specific ethnic group must include representation of those constituents in the design. Just because the strategy resonates with me or another funder does not mean it will have the desired effect on the intended audience. Sensitivity and awareness of how the target audience will receive the message is of paramount importance.

One example we funded to help understand a target audience involved SafeHaven of Tarrant County. At the time of our grant, there was only one domestic abuse shelter in all of Mexico. The Carter Foundation funded an exchange program so staff from that shelter could come see how Safe-Haven operates. More importantly, SafeHaven staff could gain an understanding of the cultural barriers that needed to be addressed to serve a woman fleeing domestic abuse from another country. ♀

PRO BONO IS NOT ALWAYS A GOOD THING

MOST NONPROFITS ARE inherently frugal because of limited resources. When professional services are needed, most look for a way to spend the least amount possible.

It is important to remember everyone has to make a living and take care of their paying customers first. People willing to do something for free are more likely to do so at the end of the day when they're tired. I would prefer nonprofits pay for the service and have the provider's full attention during the workday.

I suggest nonprofits interview several groups for any work that needs to be done. Almost without exception, at least one provider will feel a personal connection to the cause and go above and beyond in the service he or she provides.

Nonprofits should always prepare to pay for services. A pleasant surprise may result at the end of the project in the form of additional work or a contribution back to the organization. ♀

DO NOT OVERLOOK YOUR NETWORK OF CONTACTS

GOOD PHILANTHROPY OFTEN involves providing directory assistance. No one can have all the answers for every situation. However, a lifetime of experiences creates a network of people who can be a resource in a variety of areas.

The Carter Foundation has a long relationship with YES!—Youth Equipped to Succeed, a Dallas-based organization that makes group presentations to elementary, middle and high school students using age-appropriate games, object lessons, factual information, statistics and real-life stories. The students are encouraged to say yes to their dreams and goals and avoid high-risk behaviors.

One year we helped fund a video YES wanted to use in their assembly programs. They had been referred to a production studio in Colorado that had done similar work for another organization YES knew (another directory assistance example). The terrific end product delivered a humorous but serious message that resonated with the high school audience.

Separately, we assist the Women's Center with a number of initiatives. One program, *Play it Safe*, offers a series of videos to help children recognize inappropriate contact and behavior. The existing video library provided solid information but the clothing, hair styles and scenes were outdated. I connected the Women's Center with YES, which introduced the agency to the Colorado production team.

This is one example where I was glad an organization took my advice because the updated videos have proven to be popular, communicate important information and provide the Women's Center with a continuing revenue stream.

BE CAREFUL WITH FEEDBACK

No ONE CAN fund every request. As I have said here before, the Carter Foundation tries to communicate that if a proposal does not reach a priority to be considered at one of our next two meetings, we will not be able to help. I recognize receiving a declination letter from the Carter Foundation does the nonprofit no good and might even compromise their ability to secure other support.

Sometimes I'm asked what could have been done differently or what additional information should be included in future applications. I struggle with how to respond because I don't want to imply that making corrections based on my comments will cure deficiencies and lead to funding a future request. ♀

TRY NOT TO BE PARANOID, BUT OTHERS ARE WATCHING WHAT YOU FUND

BETWEEN NONPROFITS REPORTING donor support lists in Annual Reports and IRS-required public filings by foundations, other people can see what you support.

It makes sense that some organizations will reach out for support when they see a pattern of funding others in their area of interest. One year we helped complete funding to restore a rural library. When online services began reporting our grant list for that particular year, several more requests for libraries in outlying areas appeared in my mail.

I empathize with restaurants that are generous enough to offer a special meal as an auction item. There's almost a 100% chance they will be asked to do something similar for another local charity. ♀

SOMETIMES ANONYMOUS WORKS, AND SOMETIMES IT DOES NOT

Amon Carter and Nenetta Burton Carter established the Amon G. Carter Star-Telegram Employees Fund in 1949 to help Carter Publications employees who lost their homes in a catastrophic Fort Worth flood to rebuild their lives. After addressing the housing issue, sufficient funds remained to establish a supplemental pension plan for employees who outlived the length of time pension payments were allowed at the time. It also served as a medical hardship fund and scholarship program for employee children.

Carter Publications was sold in 1974, but employees at the time of sale remained eligible for benefits. Fifty-plus years later there's obviously a dwindling population. Employment Retirement Act laws were modified long ago to provide lifetime pensions, but the Employees Fund continues to assist retirees with medical hardship. Endowment assets can meet all retiree needs as well as consider other charitable community grants to reach the 5% IRS payout requirement.

We request all gifts be anonymous to avoid confusion with the Amon G. Carter Foundation, the fact the Star-Telegram is no longer involved, and that employees did not contribute to the fund.

I have noticed in Annual Reports some organizations list all anonymous contributions at the top. Others simply replace the name with "Anonymous" where it would fall in the alphabetized list.

On one occasion, the Employees Fund provided underwriting support for an event. Listed on every poster and t-shirt under Silver Sponsors was Amon G. Carter Star-Telegram Employees Fund (ANONYMOUS). ♀

GRANTMAKERS HAVE RESPONSIBILITIES

ANYONE WHO HAS ever called a doctor expects the call to be returned sooner rather than later. Funders are not in the same category as physicians (although grant applicants sometimes hope we will help them get well). My point is to never forget that this is not a level playing field and nonprofits are counting on us to communicate with them.

I encourage everyone to develop a process that acknowledges when grant requests have been received. Information should also be available describing timelines of when applications will be considered and notification received.

Try not to abide by the golden rule that says those with the gold make the rules. Always treat others with the same respect that you would expect. ♀

HARD TO DIAL BACK SUPPORT FROM A HIGHER LEVEL

MANY FUNDERS CONTRIBUTE annual support to organizations that are important to them or provide essential services in the community. The longer support is received, the more reliant the recipient will become.

The Carter Foundation tries to limit the amount of unrestricted operating support we provide. There are a number of organizations we assist on an annual basis, but we have chosen not to increase support simply because of inflation. Instead, we consider separate requests for specific, non-recurring issues. That way, once a project is completed, we can return to the lower support level without disrupting the organization's budget.

If it becomes necessary to lower the amount of historical support, I suggest giving the organization as much advance notice as possible to help them plan for replacement. ♀

DETERMINE AREAS
OF INTEREST

GRANTMAKING OPPORTUNITIES ARE limitless. Later in this book I have included several pages of funding examples that do not involve operating or capital support but might inspire other interest.

The Carter Foundation remains a broad-based funder in the categories of Education, Health, Humanities and Arts, Social Service, along with Other. We emphasize our primary service area is Fort Worth/Tarrant County, but that does not discourage a large number of grant seekers from elsewhere. As a rule, we consider requests from outside the immediate area only when they provide services to the local community or a project has potential for large-scale impact, such as medical research.

With so much information available online, it is a good idea to establish some parameters to limit the number of unsolicited requests. ♀

HAVING A NARROW FOCUS DOES NOT ENSURE FEWER REQUESTS

ONE LOCAL FOUNDATION was formed through an estate with the directive to focus on serving the hungry and homeless. I'm sure the expectation was that funding would benefit the food bank, meal delivery programs and homeless shelters.

It did not take long for creative funding opportunities to surface as other nonprofits sought ways to qualify. Ancillary requests poured in to fund services addressing this target population involving health, education, counseling, job training, temporary and permanent housing, pet food and many, many more. ♀

IN-PERSON VISITS ALWAYS
IDENTIFY OTHER ISSUES

MORE AND MORE funders rely on standardized online applications for initial contact. Even if this approach is taken, I encourage all major funding (however you define major) to include some type of face-to-face conversation.

I prefer in person, and since the overwhelming majority of our grant recipients are local there's no logistical hardship. Without exception, during the visit additional aspects of the organization will be discussed along with other challenges and opportunities.

Most Carter Foundation funding ends up a little different from the original proposal once more information around the issue is brought to light. The situation may involve fine-tuning the original ask, or the result might be something altogether different that the nonprofit never would have thought to request. ♀

VALUE OF SITE VISITS

EVEN BETTER THAN a grant discussion in a funder's conference room or on a video monitor is a site visit. Experiencing the operation in action, meeting the people doing the work, seeing the faces of those being assisted is the preferred way to understand the purpose of funding.

Nonprofit leaders are always proud to show others the work they're doing, and they will be more comfortable on their home turf. Again, on-site time together will provide the best opportunity for a grantmaker to fully grasp impact.

At some point in a site visit, nonprofits usually will hear the words they're waiting for from the funder—"I had no idea!" That means, possibly for the first time, a grantmaker is grasping the scale and magnitude of the organization's programs.

One piece of advice (warning). After seeing a program in action and the faces of those benefiting, you will want to help. ♀

THOUGHT ON STANDARDIZED APPLICATIONS

As PREVIOUSLY MENTIONED, the Carter Foundation does not have a standardized grant application. When I tell organizations this, the vast majority say, "Thank you!" I'm sure it's difficult to convey some issues in a finite number of characters. I further suspect there's a great deal of anxiety if the explanation being provided is addressing the funder's issue in question.

My son went to Rice University. Like every other institution of higher learning, the admission process began with a standardized application. In addition, Rice required every applicant to write a couple of essays. I mention this example not only as a proud parent but because the final page of the application was blank save for an empty four-inch square and the instruction, "Do something with this box." Rice used this exercise to allow students to demonstrate their creativity and personality.

Every standardized grant application form should have some type of blank page at the end for nonprofits to convey more information about themselves. ♀

PROS AND CONS OF GRANTMAKING MEETING SCHEDULES

As I POINTED out at the beginning of this portion of the book, if you have seen one grantmaking organization, you have seen one grantmaking organization. Some funders are individuals, some are family enterprises, some oversee philanthropic trusts, and others serve as foundation Directors.

There are three approaches to grantmaking. Each request is stand alone and considered as it is received. At the other end of the spectrum, all decisions are made at one meeting a year. Or requests are considered at regularly scheduled meetings throughout the year.

Considering one request at a time is the most expedient in providing an answer, but it's challenging if more than one person is involved and multiple schedules must be coordinated. If this approach is widely known, it will lead to many requests early in the funding year and the possibility of grant budgets being exhausted before other attractive opportunities arise.

Accumulating requests throughout a twelve-month period and then considering them may appear attractive because all known opportunities will be available for consideration and coordinating the meeting schedule is simplified. The downside is some requests might be almost a year old, or a time-sensitive issue might have passed. Some organizations have one major meeting a year to consider requests, and then a separate strategy to address recurring grants.

The straddle approach for many grantmakers is a series of meetings throughout the year. This allows a number of requests to be evaluated at the same time within a reasonable response time. This does require some discipline to allocate funds throughout the year along with scheduling attendance at more meetings.

Regardless of approach, a protocol should be in place to respond to an emergency or crisis in a timely manner. ♀

MULTI-YEAR COMMITMENTS

SOME PROJECTS REQUIRE multi-year commitments to ensure confidence, that there is time to complete the initiative. When the Carter Foundation makes multi-year commitments, in most situations the entire funding amount must be set aside out of the current grant budget. This funding philosophy is challenging, and most times I try to limit our commitment to two years with the understanding we will consider another grant at an appropriate time in the future.

Some organizations (including us) make multi-year commitments in order to maximize participation in a major project. There is nothing wrong with that, but we attempt to start each funding year with as much of our grant budget as possible available for new opportunities. ♀

ENCUMBERING FUTURE-YEAR GRANT BUDGETS

As just mentioned regarding multi-year grants, we try to maintain a discipline to not encumber future-year grant budgets. We do make exceptions, but there is never more than one major project at a time that will involve funding out of multiple grant budgets. With uncertainty in future-year investment performance, we do not want to wake up someday and find our funding capability limited because of previous-year unpaid commitments.

We have grants payable at the end of every year, but those amounts were set aside out of previous approved grant cycle budgets. The most common example is capital campaign commitments. The Carter Foundation often is asked for an early commitment to help signal support and create momentum for the effort. After approval, we provide written confirmation including the statement we will fund our commitment once the contract is signed to begin construction of the building.

In capital campaign situations, funding rarely occurs in the year of approval. Internally the funds are set aside out of the current-year grant budget. Whenever payment finally happens, the current year grant budget is not affected because the funds were previously encumbered. ♀

PEANUT BUTTER APPROACH

ONCE THERE WAS a very generous widow in town who was approached almost nonstop with funding requests. She told me her family started out very poor but her husband was successful and she never wanted to say no to anyone who might have been in a situation like she was early in life. It wasn't always much, but she did something for everyone who asked.

I told her that was called the peanut butter approach because she spread it around to all corners of need. She was kind to tell me she liked that analogy.

Sometimes it makes sense to divide your resources among many recipients and have your name associated with multiple endeavors. ♀

CAPACITY BUILDING

CAPACITY BUILDING IS one of the most frequently used buzz words around grantmaking. Everyone wants resources to go toward increasing the impact and doing more good work. These proposals often start with requests for expansion of advancement, development or fundraising departments.

Fundraising professionals play a critical role in furthering an organization's mission. It has been my experience that no one can be hired to make it rain—to succeed, the fundraiser must have a passion for the mission. Further, unless the development person or grant writer has a realistic strategy to raise a multiple of his or her salary from a broader base of supporters on an ongoing basis, it's not a good hire.

I always encourage new members in the development department to take notes and share with others all the things they learned since they started. If they were not aware of the information until they got there, it is likely people outside the organization wouldn't know either.

To build capacity, every employee should be considered a member of the development team. ♀

COMMUNITY FOUNDATIONS ARE WONDERFUL PARTNERS

IN ADDITION TO providing services to donor-advised funds, community foundations are strategic partners for all grant-makers. In Fort Worth, the local community foundation functions as a convener around certain issues and concerns including early childhood learning, education, and furthering philanthropy.

Frequently, with new initiatives, the North Texas Community Foundation functions as a fiscal agent until the organizations receive their IRS Determination Letter. In some instances, they continue to operate in this capacity on an ongoing basis. Examples include The Crossroads Lab Fund which provides a tax-deductible platform for the Fort Worth Star-Telegram to hire more reporters to cover the local community. Operation Progress is a public/private partnership focused on strengthening relationships with police officers and residents in select neighborhoods. The Exchange Club of Fort Worth relies on the Community Foundation to distribute donations designated to selected charities.

Community foundations also provide fiduciary oversight for the endowments of some nonprofits. Locally, they also oversee a recurring "toolbox" program that provides strategic grants to nonprofits around certain focus areas. I often refer nonprofits to the Community Foundation to help spread the word to appropriate fundholders and other funding partners interested in specific area initiatives. ♀

DEFINING SUCCESS

SUCCESS IS MORE than reaching a fundraising goal. Success also involves education, understanding and expanding the number of people involved in a movement. Regardless of the topic, having a few people simply writing checks does not define long-term success.

Further, solving a problem does not mean it will stay solved if funding goes elsewhere. In Fort Worth there was a major initiative to address the gang issue several years ago. Resources poured in and the right organizations were effective in reducing the problem to manageable levels. But once the issue was out of the news, funding was redirected to other areas and it wasn't long before the problem was back.

Success involves continuing attention, investment and awareness of the broad community. ♀

EXAMPLES OF STRATEGIC SITUATIONS TO CONSIDER

I HOPE EVERY grant I make can be considered strategic. Instead of adding another hundred pages to the book, I have included several pages listing various ways the Foundation has responded to funding opportunities. Below are several examples of what I consider strategic grants that the Carter Foundation has awarded.

Leadership Transition Funding

Social service nonprofits often start small and grow into significant community enterprises. In many instances the founder, or a longtime employee, has been responsible for overseeing the growth and complexity of the operation. This institutional knowledge is difficult to replace. In several situations the Foundation has helped fund the overlap of two CEO salaries to ensure a smooth transition. In one case the successor did not work out and the organization apologized for wasting the money. I replied that I was glad the existing executive was still involved so that there was no disruption.

Mission Increase

A number of start-up nonprofits may have one or two employees addressing emerging or niche issues. In recent years the Carter Foundation has begun funding an organization offering technical support to these small operations to help them develop strategic plans, build a Board of Directors, create budgets, establish fundraising strategies, initiate marketing plans, join a network with other providers and communicate with supporters.

Pilot Programs to Help the Foundation Learn

The Carter Foundation made a grant to help create an out-door wireless communication system. We wanted not only to assist with this cultural installation but to use this as an opportunity to learn what works, provide better advice and evaluate requests for similar technology projects.

In another situation the Foundation funded a pilot program that offered financial incentives for veterans completing a series of six counseling sessions. The study was intended to compare outcomes of those attending all sessions versus others not completing the full course of treatment.

Programs Where the Outcomes are Already Known

Studies confirm that 30% of low-income children have undiagnosed vision issues. The Foundation has been an ongoing supporter of a vision van that goes to schools and provides eye exams for all students pre-screened as potentially needing correction. After evaluation, students may select a frame and receive prescription glasses free of charge the same day.

Win-Win for Students and Schools

Communities in Schools provides case management for students identified as being at risk for dropping out. These school-based interventionists are CIS employees and school districts and private dollars each cover half of the salaries. Since school districts receive funding based on attendance, it is in their best interest for students to be present in school. Since Communities in Schools works with the population most in danger of quitting, every student served is progressing toward graduation and the school district is maximizing revenue. ♀

OTHER TYPES OF GRANT IDEAS FOR CONSIDERATION

IN ADDITION TO operating support and capital campaigns, here are some other grantmaking ideas. This list highlights different types of grants the Amon G. Carter Foundation has made.

EDUCATION

Campus master planning

Collaborative projects among institutions

Community-wide reading initiatives

Conference and/or guest speaker underwriting

Continuing education for professional development

Curriculum development

Curriculum purchase

Discretionary funds for university presidents and chancellors

Distance learning projects

Establish distance learning production studios

Facility assessments

Facility improvements

Graduate instruction for principal training

Library program to digitize archives

Marketing support

Matching grants to improve public school athletic facilities

Outdoor play area enhancement

(Continued) Other Types of Grant Ideas for Consideration: Education

Pilot program to help retain first-generation college students

Program evaluation for effectiveness

Public charter school advocacy

Purchase laptop computers

Purchase musical instruments

Scholarship support

Science and engineering competitions

School district education foundation support for innovative initiatives

School district trustee training

School of social work research projects

Share best practices for parent engagement

Sliding scale support for evaluation and/or tutoring

Speaker series underwriting

Special event underwriting

Strategic planning support

Student recruitment programs

Summer enrichment program for promising students

Technology support

Travel support to visit colleges where accepted and offered scholarships

University research programs

Volunteer mentor program

Year zero funding for charter school start-up hiring and marketing

HEALTH AND MEDICINE

Adolescent and young adult oncology support services

Aircraft maintenance for medical usage

Alzheimer's disease research

Autism services

Biomedical research

Blind individuals work programs

Blindness prevention

Breast cancer program support

Camps for children with specific medical conditions

Cancer research using DNA mapping

Canine companion training

Community health service facility support

Community surveys identifying service gaps

Continuing education for medical professionals

Continuing education for mental health providers

Coordinate volunteer physicians and nurses

Defibrillator program for rural law enforcement

Dental health

Diabetes research

Emergency department pilot program addressing frequent users

Establish charitable healthcare clinics

Event underwriting

Food preparation program to promote healing and recovery

Glioblastoma research

Healthcare clinics for the underserved

Hospice program focused on children

Hospital employee scholarships for those identified for advancement

Immunization program for the community

Insurance program underwriting to continue treatment

Leukemia and lymphoma support programs

Marketing program promoting blood donations

Medical mission trips

Medical supplies needed by paraplegics and quadriplegics

Mental health program to coordinate community services

Mobile outreach to homeless camps

Mother's milk bank

Music therapy for dementia patients

Nurse training programs

Palliative care interview capture using artificial intelligence

Patient satisfaction research

Pediatric cancer research

Pilot programs for hospice and palliative care

Pregnancy center equipment

Prescription assistance training for pharmaceutical-subsidized application forms

Program supporting providers of attendant care to home-bound individuals

Research funding for promising discoveries

Respiratory research

Retina research

Shaken baby expert witness program

Simulation training for physicians and nurses

(Continued) Other Types of Grant Ideas for Consideration: Health and Medicine

Sliding scale support for evaluation programs

Therapeutic riding support

Training community leaders to disseminate information

Vision screening program reaching low-income population (along with providing glasses)

Way-finding improvements to assist patients navigating facilities

HUMANITIES AND ARTS

Career management of performers

Children's education programs

Coordination of a cultural group's efforts

Demonstration project underwriting

Enhance walking and biking trails

Musical instrument program purchase

Performing groups' lighting, sound and wireless microphone needs

Public library assisting students with college essays and applications

Publication support

Relocate administrative offices

Renovate historic properties

Replace operating support during endowment campaign

Roadway beautification

Sizzle reel to promote a project concept

Statue refurbishing

Strategic planning

(Continued) Other Types of Grant Ideas for Consideration: Humanities and Arts

Support acquisition for land conservation
Ticket software with dynamic pricing
Traveling exhibit underwriting
Upgrade public broadcasting technology
Wetlands restoration

SOCIAL SERVICES

After-school reading enrichment using retired teachers
Air conditioning for camp housing
Airport chaplaincy program
Airport respite areas for military
Art therapy
Bereavement counseling for children
Children's advocacy
Disaster preparedness
Educational video underwriting
Emergency response infrastructure
Employment program start-up
Engineering evaluation/assessment of facilities
Group home remodeling
Guardianship services
Home improvements for families recovering from serious surgeries
Insurance deductible payments
Intern program expansion
Leadership transition underwriting
Legal services to improve neighborhoods

(Continued) Other Types of Grant Ideas for Consideration: Social Services

Legal services for those who cannot afford

Little League facility improvements

Marriage enrichment

Mental health counseling in schools

Mentorship programming

Merger underwriting

Office relocation

Outcome measurement

Parenting publications

Pet food bank

Police/community relations

Prison programs offering education and training

Property purchase assistance

School dropout prevention

Security enhancements to facilities

Sliding scale support for clients/patients

Speaker underwriting

Suicide and crisis support

Summer enrichment programs

Technology support for a broadcast studio

Training program for injured veterans

Transition to group employment/benefit provider

Transportation repairs for low-income workers

Veterans support

Warehouse shelving for food pantries

OTHER

Business incubators

College campus programs

Community foundation initiatives

Community redevelopment

Drowning prevention training

Economic development

Giving day incentives

Historic preservation

Junior League projects

Leadership training

Nonprofit board training

Nonprofit consulting services

Nonprofit news service

Police and fire department initiatives

Promoting the city

Promoting volunteerism

Public policy research

Public/private partnerships

Radio podcasts

Spay and neutering services for pet adoptions

Statewide planning ♀

FREQUENTLY ASKED QUESTIONS

What expectations do you have of yourself as a grantmaker?

- During every meeting my goal is to ask at least one question or offer a perspective the nonprofit's leaders have not considered, even though they wake up every day focused on that area of interest.

- I try to emphasize aspects of their project I believe others would like to know more about but might not ask. Hopefully, this can improve future presentations and help them succeed with other funders.

- I often provide "directory assistance" regarding who else the organization should approach about partnerships or support.

- I also suggest any other supporting documents they need to have available in case someone asks.

What are hallmarks of effective nonprofit organizations?

- Leadership capable of anticipating and responding to ever-changing markets, environments and personnel challenges.

- Leaders who can communicate how and why their programs remain relevant and are working.

- Operational funding is stable or at least offers a strategy with reasonable potential for success.

- Foundation and/or trust funding is used for strategic initiatives or expansion.
- Willing to admit when things are not working and what course corrections need to be made.
- Other organizations look to them to participate in appropriate partnerships or initiatives

What factors do you consider when evaluating a grant request?

- Since I have a financial background, I always ask for prior year budgets, prior year actuals and current year budgets to evaluate reasonableness
- Who/what need is being addressed and what is the expected impact?
- Is the service unique?
- Do other providers (and users) value what is being offered?
- Does the organization have a reputation for doing what they say they are going to do?
- Is there a sustainability plan that does not include me?

Can a grant ever be harmful?

- A gift that is so large that it covers too much of the operational expenses might send the signal that other donors do not need to participate because the one funder is so heavily invested that they will not let the project fail.

- Oversized grants can lessen the urgency to generate broader support.
- Excess funding potentially can enable/mask poor management.
- Grants that are too large or are received at the wrong time can set up an organization for failure if sustainability is not addressed.

What different funding strategies do you use?

- We make very few general unrestricted operating grants. This type of funding is usually modest and provides support for organizations we want our names associated with every year.
- Most of our grants target specific project requests to advance the organization's mission.
- Every year a few grants are larger and usually involve capital improvements.
- Some grants are intended to promote social enterprise through entrepreneurial philanthropy to help groups help themselves.
- Specific funding goes toward stimulating interest around an issue or problem by convening multiple groups to work together.
- Non-recurring situations are funded to assist with consultants, master planning and facilitating merger discussions.
- Separate funding is set aside to address discretionary and emergency situations
- Read the first half of this book!

What are three things you look for to analyze the effectiveness of an organization?

- Uniqueness, population served and impact.

- Reputation for meeting promised outcomes.

- What clients and other service providers think about the organization's contribution to the community.

When is it a good idea to fund general operations?

- If the organization is important to you and you want your name associated with them on an ongoing basis.

- When you recognize there will always be a need and you're willing to fund at a similar level indefinitely.

- To emphasize the importance of the core service to others in the community.

- To address a temporary/emergency gap in funding.

- When plans exist to activate other funding streams in the future.

Should a nonprofit ever admit failure?

- Hopefully there is enough rapport that the organization feels comfortable being honest and transparent regarding their situation.

- I want to know what happened—good and bad.

- During a pilot project, the most important thing is lessons learned—what is working and what course corrections need to be made.

If I only have the same amount of funds to give away each year, how can I do a better job?

- If you're comfortable with what you support, stay the course, no change is necessary.

- Do not overlook your potential to provide leverage through your gift (if you have a relationship with the organization).

- At all support levels the potential exists to assist with less attractive needs, thus freeing others to address ongoing funding situations.

As a grantmaker, if you were in a nonprofit's shoes, what issues would drive you crazy?

- How to get an audience and what to ask for.
- Not knowing the true status of a grant request.
- How decisions are really made.
- By what method and how often to communicate.
- How to acknowledge and whom to thank.

What are some warning signs a grant is not warranted at this time?

- Inadequate planning, insufficient information, uncertain funding sources.

- Inability to answer questions, thus creating a lack of confidence.

- Unclear demand for program services and potential outcomes.

- No articulated plan to secure other funding.
- No strategy to sustain operations.

Not everything you have funded has worked. What mistakes have you made?

Two mistakes (that I will admit to) involve people.

- I had the bright idea to co-locate several small non-profits so they could share a receptionist, break room, conference room, and provide emotional support for one another since they all dealt with very challenging issues. I thought the most established nonprofit with the largest budget would be the logical choice to take the lead and be responsible for the lease and shared personnel. It turned out the person in that leadership position was not the right manager for this situation. By the time I found out, the lease had been canceled for nonpayment and the organizations had gone their separate ways.

- I was working with a community group in a low-income neighborhood. That group needed operating support, which was not a good fit for me. I asked about other revenue sources and the director told be about a home renovation program the organization had with the city. They received abandoned houses with clear titles after back taxes were waived and it was confirmed no heirs had claim to the property. The organization had a construction manager who was very good at renovating the houses (on budget) and getting them ready for resale. The Foundation provided a pool of funds so more houses could be renovated and returned to the neighborhood. Net profit from each sale could be used to support other program operations. This worked fine until the construction manager decided he could make more money working on his own renovation projects. The organization never could find a replacement to line up the subcontractors and complete the projects on budget. Eventually all of the renovation pool funds were expended. ♀

A LESSON LEARNED
THE HARD WAY

THIS EXAMPLE IS not about a grant that went wrong but instead a grant recommendation that never got approved. Early in my grantmaking career, I met with representatives of Westworth Village. This municipality, adjacent to Fort Worth, was being deeded a golf course that had been part of the property owned by an Air Force base.

Plans were for the golf course to become a public amenity for the community and also generate revenue by hosting golf tournaments. The one thing missing was a covered pavilion with tables and chairs to accommodate pre-round check-in, meals and post-round award ceremonies.

The request to the Carter Foundation was for $75,000 to pour a concrete slab and build a metal roof shade structure. In return, the Foundation was offered five charity golf tournament days completely free—no greens fees, no cart cost, no food or beverage cost. Charities designated by the Foundation would keep 100% of the money raised.

This sounded like a fantastic way to help Westworth Village with golf course improvements plus enable each of the five Foundation Board members to designate a favorite charity to help raise some money. I figured any charity could raise at least $50,000 if they had no cost other than event publicity. Five events raising $50,000 would result in $250,000 being raised in return for a $75,000 grant.

Well, the Board declined my recommendation. It never occurred to me to inquire whether anyone liked the idea. Looking back, the Foundation had never expected (or accepted) anything in return for a grant. I also had not considered the optics surrounding the idea. Having each Board member choose a "favorite" charity would have been awkward and not a good look.

The Board was right and I was wrong to pursue this one-time idea. From that Board meeting on, we modified our approach to not repeat the situation.

The following few pages provide a glimpse of how the Carter Foundation prepares for a Board meeting. But remember, if you have seen one foundation, you have seen one foundation. ♀

AMON CARTER
FOUNDATION APPROACH

Discussion Meeting

I MAINTAIN A worksheet to keep track of every organization I meet with and every grant request I receive that meets a certain criteria for consideration. I do not include on this consideration document unsolicited grants from other areas of the country or from around the world.

The worksheet separates requests into the areas of: Education, Health and Medicine, Humanities and Arts, Social Services, and Other. Each area is further divided into capital projects and more modest requests.

The Carter Foundation has three Board meetings a year where we conduct business activity, review investment performance and consider grant requests. To make Board meetings as productive as possible, a discussion meeting is held three weeks prior to review grant requests for consideration.

Each discussion meeting starts with an overview of all capital campaigns in the area. I prioritize those to be considered at the upcoming meeting, those anticipated for future meetings, and those less likely to make an agenda. Given our funding discipline not to encumber future grant meetings, much of the conversation centers on, "If we commit to this project now, we will have to postpone a decision on this one." I also use the discussion meeting to make the Board aware of "opportunities" not yet publicly announced but for which planning is underway.

After the capital project discussion, we review the operating requests that have been prioritized for the upcoming Board meeting along with any already planned for the next meeting. The discussion meeting is also an opportunity for Board members to ask about projects not prioritized or to raise questions concerning projects they have heard or read about from other sources.

By the end of the meeting, the goal is for everyone to have a clear understanding of the projects moving forward for consideration at the Board meeting. The objective is for the lights to be green so that all agenda items can be approved at the proposed level. ♀

AMON CARTER FOUNDATION APPROACH

Preparation for Board Meeting

PREPARATION OF THE agenda and packet of information for the Board meeting begins in earnest after the discussion meeting. The Carter Foundation Board has chosen not to evaluate the entire grant request submission but instead receive a one-page synopsis of each project along with the recommended funding amount.

My preparation of these summaries is intended to be concise and address all questions raised during the discussion meeting. Each page starts with the organization name on top and an italicized recommendation for funding and brief program description. The remainder of the page gives background on the organization and rationale for funding the project along with expected outcomes.

As our process has evolved, I find these one-page summaries to be an efficient way to remind the Board members of our discussion meeting conversation and help them get through the fifty or so requests to be considered. These summaries are also a good way to chronicle our grant activity for future reference.

The final reason I prepare these one-page recommendations is in case another funder wants to know what we're doing and why. In addition to justifying my recommendations to the Carter Foundation Board, I want to help advocate and build a case for other funders to consider support. ♀

AMON CARTER
FOUNDATION APPROACH

Board Packet

MOST BOARD MEETINGS are on Tuesdays. Each Board member receives a notice two weeks in advance, and a bound packet is delivered the Friday before the meeting containing:

- Agenda
- Minutes from the prior meeting
- Details of all business activity requiring Board approval
- Investment results
- Current status of Amon Carter Museum funding
- Summary of grant funds available along with detail of grants paid during the year and those still unpaid
- Summary page of all grant recommendations by category (Education, Health and Medicine, Humanities and Arts, Social Services, Other)
- One-page narrative of each recommendation

On the summary page, under each category, the organizations appear in alphabetical order along with a page reference for the recommendation and funding amount. Following the summary page, the one-page synopsis for each organization is ordered starting with the largest amount being recommended. We have recently added a funding history of amounts to the organization on the page opposite the recommendation. ♀

AMON CARTER
FOUNDATION APPROACH

Board Meeting

THE PRESIDENT DETERMINES a quorum, entertains a motion to approve the minutes, and guides the Board through all agenda business and investment items with input from appropriate staff.

The grant recommendations typically occupy the largest portion of the meeting. Each request is considered independently. After discussion and questions, each recommendation requires a motion, second and majority approval for funding.

I especially appreciate the strict adherence at these Board meetings to the published agenda. We easily could fall into the habit of introducing additional funding considerations. We have found the discussion meeting the best time to address any other potential issues.

The next discussion meeting and Board meeting dates are set before adjournment and published on our website. ♀

AMON CARTER
FOUNDATION APPROACH

Summarized

Prospective grant recipient

- Call for an appointment before submitting a request.

- Allow as much time as possible before needing an answer.

- Review, summarize and include previous year's budget, previous year's actual results, and current year budget, highlighting anticipated changes.

- Tell us about all of your programs and needs, not just the one you think will be of interest.

- Explore entrepreneurial opportunities and how we can help you help yourself.

- Remember, everyone we talk to needs support, and we want to make our impact go as far as possible.

Overview

- Funding is balanced between Education, Health and Medicine, Humanities and Arts, Social Services, and Other.

- Only approve commitments out of current year's budget.

- Usually have mixture of capital, challenge, program expansion and minimal operating.

- No grants get funded solely through a letter request or contact with a Director.

- Directors hold a discussion meeting in advance of the Board meeting to set grant agenda.

- All recommendations on the grant agenda can be approved.

- Three grant meetings: February, May and November.

- I prepare a lead schedule by category of all grant recommendations, including amounts.

- One-page synopsis of each grant recommendation from highest to lowest amount.

- Notification of approval and funding timeline is reported by telephone after meeting. ♀

CONCLUSION

6 R's of Effective Grantmaking

I APPRECIATE ANYONE willing to consider my thoughts on grantmaking. I have been asked many times to speak on effective fundraising so I developed six rules for that. I have never been asked to speak on effective *grantmaking*, but since I wrote this book to provide an overview of my approach, here are my corollaries to effective fundraising—the 6 R's of Effective Grantmaking:

1) **Research**

   Grantmakers need to learn as much as they can about the requesting organizations and their programs, leadership, financial results and reputation among other nonprofits.

2) **Relationships**

   Getting to know the people who run the operation being funded is essential. I cannot imagine making a grant decision based on nothing more than an application received in the mail, or just online.

3) **Real Estate**

   There is no substitute for seeing an organization in action. In addition to being on site, the nonprofit's leaders will be more comfortable—and proud!—to show what they do rather than having to describe it as they sit in a funder's imposing conference room.

4) **Rationale**

Grantmaking should always be strategic. By choosing from a menu of options, funding can be directed toward areas of interest and where you feel it will have the most impact.

5) **Realistic**

Be candid in guiding organizations on what funding level is reasonable for their request.

6) **Report Back**

To help manage expectations, it's always good to let organizations know when decisions will be made and how future communication will be handled. ♀

R.F.I.

Request for Inspiration

I HOPE THAT everyone reading this book will think of several ways these ideas can translate to organizations, causes, or strategies they can use. My request to you is to please share any inspirations you get from this book along with the results and forward it to www.myinspiration@yournextinspiration.com.

Who knows, your inspiration might be highlighted and inspire someone else in a future sequel! ♀

DEDICATION

To those who inspire me every day:
Charlotte
Marshall
Pamela
Stephen
Ashley
Margot
Kelly
Christopher
Carter

SPECIAL THANKS

To those who encouraged me and
helped this book idea become a reality:
Dave Lieber
Rose Bradshaw
Chip Flaherty
John Dycus
Tamara Dever
Monica Thomas